Home Bound

Growing Up with a
Disability in America

CASS IRVIN

TEMPLE UNIVERSITY PRESS
Philadelphia

TO MY DADDY, MELVIN C. IRVIN

Temple University Press, Philadelphia 19122
Copyright © 2004 by Cass F. Irvin
All rights reserved
Published 2004
Printed in the United States of America

⊗The paper used in this publication meets the requirements of the American
National Standard for Information Sciences—Permanence of Paper for Printed
Library Materials, ANSI Z39.48-1984

Library of Congress Cataloging-in-Publication Data

Irvin, Cass, 1945–
    Home bound : growing up with a disability in America / Cass Irvin.
        p. cm.
    ISBN 1-59213-219-7 (cloth : alk. paper) — ISBN 1-59213-220-0 (pbk. : alk. paper)
    1. Irvin, Cass, 1945—Health.   2. Quadriplegics–Kentucky–Biography.
3. Poliomyelitis–Patients–Kentucky–Biography.   I. Title.
RC406.Q33I785 2004
362.1'96835'0092—dc21
[B]   2003050789

2   4   6   8   9   7   5   3   1

Home Bound

Growing Up with a Disability in America

Contents

Acknowledgments

In 1995, after a long afternoon of advocacy training, I poured out my frustrations about the lack of strong disability advocacy in my community to a friend, Mary Johnson, editor of *The Disability Rag*. She asked, "Well, what do you want to do about it?" "I want to write a book!" I answered. "Okay," she responded. "Let's find out how to do it." And we did.

While the observations and the conclusions herein are mine, they were generated from the experiences of many people. I have learned from them and have tried to tell the stories as we lived them.

I have been influenced strongly by my experience working for and growing up with *The Disability Rag*, a magazine that has become a vehicle for developing disability thinkers and writers. Some of the stories in this book first saw print in the pages of *The Disability Rag* and *Ragged Edge* magazines.

Betty Friedan's *Feminine Mystique* encouraged me to write my own book. She gave words to my pain and aloneness, to my problem with no name. Her book sent me racing toward the women's movement; I found solace and sisterhood there. I hope I have been able to interpret the feminist philosophy properly from a disability perspective.

I would not have been able to write *Home Bound* without the support of the Kentucky Foundation for Women, Inc., and its founder, Sallie Bingham. The Kentucky Foundation for Women is one of the few foundations in the country that provides grants to feminist artists. Without grant support, I would not have had personal assistants to help me take this book from tapes to text to manuscript. The foundation's confidence in my work made me feel like a real artist, and I am extremely grateful to them.

Juanita Redman was my housekeeper and personal assistant when I began writing the book; she was "my arms and legs" when it came to copying, mailing, running errands, and doing anything else I needed in the office. John Garrett, my love and life partner, has been involved from the beginning. He helped run Access to the Arts, Inc., when I was too "into the book" to do everything, and he smoothed the path to being a published author with moral support and love.

I want to thank Temple University Press and, especially, Janet Francendese, my editor, who never gave up on this once inexperienced writer. And I must thank my agent and friend, David Zinman, who put his energy behind my dream.

The last person I want to thank is also the first person I need to thank: Mary Johnson, my "significant other" in disability and one of my best friends. Over twenty-five years ago she showed me that the personal is political and introduced me to a vehicle— ALPHA, Inc., a disability advocacy organization—so I could do something about change. She made writing truly accessible to me and started me on this infamous writing career.

1   From the Kitty Room

Ourselves, our lives, our times, our truths, our culture. Do we collect it all
piece by painful piece, or do we invent it? Does it matter? We've patched
together our lives after years of disability, and now we're patching together
our culture after decades of fragmentation. We're reinventing ourselves
personally, and now we're doing it collectively.
—Barry Corbet, "Art and Life"

I BELIEVE I have finally made the circle. I fled from this
little bedroom in my parents' home to live my own life when I
was twenty-nine. I came back to this house in 1984, but it has
taken me years to get to the point where I could feel comfortable
coming back to this room.

Sometimes I think my whole life has been a journey to find
out where my place is. For a long time, I didn't realize everyone
is on such a journey. I thought other people, people who were
not disabled, had it all figured out—that it was only I who didn't
know where I fit in. Because I was different.

I learned when I was growing up that if you were a girl, you
went to school, then college, and then you married, became a
wife, and had a family. (I grew up before Betty Friedan wrote *The
Feminine Mystique*.) When I became disabled, my journey, I was
pretty sure, was not meant to take me in those directions. So I
tried to find my place. What was I supposed to be? What kind of
life was I supposed to have?

The role models I had were President Franklin D. Roosevelt,
who had polio like I did and who was successful and was a hero
for a whole nation; Elizabeth Barrett Browning, a romantic poet

The epigraph is from Barry Corbet, "Art and Life," *New Mobility*, August 1998.

1

who was considered an invalid and was "rescued" by poet Robert Browning when he whisked her away from her oppressive father and began with her one of the most famous courtships in literature; and Tiny Tim from Charles Dickens's *A Christmas Carol*, who was poor and humble and all-forgiving.

I knew from the beginning that if you were handicapped but had money, class, and stature, you could be like Roosevelt or Browning and have a good life. But if you were poor, you were Tiny Tim—or the little boy in elementary school I gave my sandwich to. He had wooden crutches and braces and worn-out brown high-top shoes. He was skinny and looked hungry. He was "crippled." At that time, I was not. When I gave him part of my sandwich, Mom fussed at me for giving away my lunch. After I became handicapped, I was afraid I might end up like him.

I was lucky, because my parents could afford a handicapped child. I thought we were rich, but I did not have enough experience to be sure what rich was. We had a nice house in the south end of Louisville. Building was just beginning out here, and it was not a rich area, so land was inexpensive. My parents bought three-fourths of an acre on Kenwood Hill near Iroquois Park.

I think my family was pretty normal for the times. Both my parents were depression-era kids, even though the depression affected them in different ways. My mom came from a "good family," although her father made some of his money from taverns. My dad's family was poor. He worked during high school. He graduated third in his class, and he liked to point out that he was the youngest of the three top graduates. He worked through college and paid his own way. Since my dad's family consisted of preachers or women who married preachers, his mom was not too keen on my maternal grandfather's business. I never looked down on it. Because of Paw-Paw's taverns and other property, my mom had a comfortable life—and was even a little stuck-up.

Maw-Maw, my maternal grandmother, told me stories about taking care of her first child (Mom) and cooking all morning in their apartment above the tavern. She would cook tongue for sandwiches and a big pot of soup and then have to carry it all downstairs for the workers who came in for lunch. When I was a little girl, I was impressed that Paw-Paw never allowed un-escorted woman in the tavern. I also bragged to my elementary school classmates that my grandfather could drink half a case of beer in a day. I didn't know that this was a pretty good indication of alcoholism.

My mom and dad met in college. Daddy was studying to be a chemist and Mom was studying to be a lawyer, which was what her dad wanted her to be. When she finally stood up for herself, she switched fields and became a teacher. She and Daddy got jobs after college, married, moved into an apartment, and began saving for a house. Typical for the pre-war 1940s.

When they bought land for the house, Mother and Daddy cleared it themselves, drew up the plans for the house, and designed many of the features inside. Mom used to talk about how she got a bad case of poison ivy from burning the rubbish they cleared; the poison ivy was in the smoke and got all over her. We always gasped when she told the story of Daddy falling through to the living room ceiling while trying to put insulation in the attic floor. He didn't get hurt. Their youth and pioneering spirit impressed me. As I look back, I realize that most of that pioneering was to save money. Still, it was impressive.

I judged all homes by this house. The first time I went to a friend's house to play, I was shocked that their house was so small. I remember thinking it would be unpleasant to live there. But I never thought we were rich because we had a big house. In fact, I often felt we were kind of poor, because the basement was unfinished and the upstairs had an unfinished attic and a tiny bedroom my sister, Ann, and I shared. If our bedroom was any indicator, I was sure, we were poor.

The room barely held two beds and two kids' tiny desks and chairs, although we did have a big walk-in closet (before they were trendy). We also had a metal furnace grate on the floor. On cold winter days I would stand on it until I felt its crisscross marks being branded on the bottoms of my socked feet. I wouldn't get off even when my feet began to hurt badly, because I knew that soon, too soon, the furnace would go off and my billowing white cotton slip would slowly collapse around my legs and I'd be cold. I never understood how it could get that cold that fast.

In 1954, when I was nine years old, I got polio at Girl Scout camp. It was an epidemic at that time. When I became sick, the camp nurse called Mom. Mom thought it was just homesickness (and I was homesick too!) so she said, "Let's just wait a day or two." The next morning when the camp nurse came to check on me I was sitting with my arms propped behind me. The pose was a classic symptom of polio. She was distraught that she had not discovered me sooner.

After a six months' hospital stay, I was able to come home. I could not walk anymore, so I couldn't go back to the room upstairs I shared with my sister. I moved into the room beside the kitchen. It had been a nursery, then Daddy's den, and was now occupied by my four-year-old brother, M.C.

When it was a den, the piano was there, and Daddy's desk with his pipes and pipe rack, and his glass ashtray with the rubber tire around it from some convention. One wall was covered with *Esquire* magazine cartoons—Mom edged them with black tape so they look framed. The room also had three corner windows. When my brother was born, it became a nursery again.

When I saw my brother for the first time he was in his crib crying. I was able to quiet him, and I felt maternal. When he was two, I had to pick him up and remove him from the presence of a "no-no" and he was mad and kicked me in the shins. I decided then that I did not want children.

Some might think it was kind of weird sharing a room with your little brother, but it was good for me—it meant I didn't have to be alone. We grew close because we lived in the same room for a couple of years and we depended on each other. At different times in my life, I have depended on him too much. I think we all have.

After I had polio, I spent a lot of time being rehabilitated at the Roosevelt Institute at Warm Springs, Georgia; it was the "in" place for people who had polio. I did not realize until years later that most kids around Louisville went to the city's Kosair Crippled Children's Hospital for rehabilitation. I'm not sure why I got to go to Warm Springs, but friends tell me we must have been rich because only rich people could afford to go there. I was sure we were not rich, because Daddy always talked about how expensive it was to travel, and I know we had financial help from the March of Dimes.

When I remember the times I was unafraid and unalone as a child, I find those times were at Warm Springs. Until then, my mother had kept pointing out to me that I was different from most handicapped kids, so I hadn't associated with them. It is a paradox that an institution can be liberating, but for me Warm Springs was. Life was accessible to me there. There I learned about life with a disability and how to get along in the world—life lessons.

Home was different. There were lots of activities Mom had to stop participating in, because even though I was nine and small for my age, a handicapped child—any age, any size—is a burden. Sometimes Mom liked to use me as an excuse: "Well, you see, I have this handicapped child at home so, no, I cannot bake cakes for the school festival."

When I was ten years old, my sister, Ann, told me that the reason Mom drank so much was because she had to take care of me. I was too much work for her, my sister said. I shouldn't ask for so much. My sister was twelve. What did she know? But that experience, plus my mother's "weak stomach" and her distaste for all bodily functions taught me early on not to ask for too much from her. I tried to make life easier for others. My aunts complimented me on the fact that I never complained, never felt sorry for myself; I was praised for having adjusted to my handicap. And so I learned that people like you better when you make few demands on them.

What my child's mind could not realize was that my mother's inability to care for me had more to do with her disability (alcoholism) than with mine. I did not leave the room for months because it was more convenient for her if I didn't. I remember noting in my diary that I had spent thirty days in my room. In my bed, actually. I knew that was significant, although I did not know I had become "bedridden." It was just easier on my mom if I did not get in my wheelchair.

When I was about eleven, a social worker came to visit to discuss a March of Dimes event. As she sat with me and my mom in my room, she remarked on our house ("How beautiful!") and said she could tell just by talking to me that my parents were educated—that showed in how articulate I was. She told me I was very lucky to have parents who cared. Many kids she visited were poor and dirty; their moms couldn't take care of them.

I was educated in this room from fifth grade through high school except for one class when I was a junior. The schools called the program Home Instruction for the Homebound. I called it "home tutoring," because that sounded prestigious. It was an inadequate education. How much can you learn in two hours, one day a week? I missed most of the typical experiences of adolescence because I was in this room instead of in school—although from all I've heard about adolescence, I'm glad I missed them!

Finally, my senior year, I got to go to school all day (actually four hours a day, because that's all the credits I needed).

By this time Daddy had hired a maid to help Mom; her name was Chris. She was black. She started coming to the house two days a week, then three days a week; then, when I got to go back to regular school, she came every weekday. Five days a week she helped me get bathed, dressed, up in my wheelchair, and out of the house. She became my second mom, although I didn't realize that until years later.

On my first day at high school the girls' counselor introduced me to Ruth, the only other visibly handicapped student in my class. The counselor thought we would be fast friends. Ruth had a big family, was from the country, and was poor. She had had polio too, but she could walk. Only one leg was affected; she limped. The cause of our disability was the only thing we had in common—yet we did become friends.

Ruth and I were pretty much accepted by our classmates. Ruth was smart, hardworking, and involved with school activities and church. I was accepted probably because I wasn't there long enough for people to get to know me well enough to find fault with me. I was learning, though, that part of being handicapped is being different. And being different in high school is hard. You know you are different—and you know you cannot do much about it. You cannot cure it. You cannot change it. The only solace is knowing it is not your fault.

But the proms were difficult. I went to the junior-senior prom when I was a junior, because the juniors gave the dance for the seniors. Since I was working at the reception table, it looked okay not to have a date. Ruth worked at the reception table, too. Maw-Maw made my dress; it was blue taffeta with spaghetti straps and white eyelet lace over the skirt. She also made a lace jacket to cover my shoulders. I got my hair done the day before and tried to sleep on it without messing it up. I was not successful.

Daddy drove me to the prom and Ruth's brother drove her. It was in a big, posh hotel downtown, and during the prom, Daddy went to dinner with one of his good-looking bachelor friends. When they came to pick Ruth and me up, Daddy's handsome friend asked Ruth to dance, which made her night!

I did not go to my senior prom because I did not have a date. Two junior girls asked me a week before the prom if I would like to help them at the reception table. I told them I was busy that night. I wasn't.

High school was a defining place for me. I was different not only because I was handicapped but also because I had not been to

formal school for five years. During those years of home instruction—even though I never got more than halfway through any
textbook—I still made all As and Bs.

When I got to "real" school, I was eager to find out how I mea-
sured up to normal kids. You know how important it is for college, stature, and ego to be in the top ten? In a class of 110, I
was number 11. I wanted to feel sad that I had gotten so close and
missed, until I realized the rankings were based on grades, and my
grades did not accurately reflect my educational achievements.
My education had not been the same as my classmates'.

I was smart enough to go to college. I lived at home, in this
room, and Chris drove me back and forth. Mom finally admitted
she could not do it. Well, she did not actually admit it, but she did
say she could be doing other things with the time. Like resting.

I went to college in the late Sixties—that era of liberation.
Thank God I didn't go to our local university! I would have been
lost on the huge campus, let alone among the masses of people,
the large, old buildings, the steps! Instead I went to a small, accessible Baptist college. It opened in 1962 and closed in 1969. Long
enough for me to come out of my back room and grow and spread
my wings and begin to become my own person—at last.

During my third year in college, I wrote for the school newspaper, was vice president of the art club and president of the literary
club (politics got me there), and a part of the group that had the
first dance held on campus. The downside to these extracurricular events was that I had to depend on my dad for transportation.
It was kind of humiliating to be one of two people in my college
whose fathers drove us to ball games and lit club meetings and
such. Of course, for me, it was understandable—I was a cripple.
The other girl who shared this humiliation was a missionary's
daughter; she was not allowed to go anywhere on her own.

I even lived in a dorm during my sophomore year, with the help
of two dorm mates and with Chris coming to my dorm two days
a week. And with Daddy, of course, paying the bills. I could do
almost anything as long as I had help.

After college I tried for a couple of years to get a job teaching. Not one public or private school in the area would hire me—a teacher in a wheelchair. For several more years I tried to get other jobs, but no luck. I was in my late twenties, living at home with my mom and dad. My sister and brother had long since grown up and moved out. I was still here, unemployed and miserable.

I lived in this room and looked out the window at night and realized that, even though I was very lucky, I had missed a lot. I used my wheelchair only when I went out. The rest of the time, I was in bed. Not asleep, not incapacitated or sick. Just—in bed. Staying there just made everything easier.

A red sticker with a big black "I" pasted on our front door let firefighters know that inside, there was a handicapped person, an "invalid." I knew intellectually it did not label me "not valid," but some days I felt that way.

I lived in this room and looked out the window at night and prayed and cried and wished things would be better. I wished Mom would stop drinking or Daddy would be home more—except Mom drank more when he was home.

Sometimes when she fell and no one was here but me, I wished she would not get up. Or sometimes I wished Daddy would die and Mom would not have any reason to drink anymore and she would be able to take care of me and she would like me better.

A harsh truth began to emerge: Most of the negative elements in my life were caused by my parents' problems. I had to get out of this room, out of this house. If this is all I will ever have, I don't want to be here, I thought. I considered killing myself.

A college friend, a social worker, suggested I go to a family counselor. This was not a foreign idea to me. I minored in psychology and I had gone to counseling in college. Now, with the counselor's help, I discovered it was possible for me to live elsewhere with a companion, as I came to call my personal care attendant. And for ten years I lived away. I lived in some neat places around Louisville: in the historic Cherokee Triangle area;

on a horse farm in Prospect, Kentucky; at a landscape nursery in Lyndon, Kentucky

Even when I moved out of my parents' house into my own apartment and got a motorized wheelchair, I stayed in bed a lot, for I had learned that some people can be more productive, more functional, in bed. These bedrooms, though, were very different from the one I stayed in at my parents' house. In every rented apartment, in every house, I claimed the biggest room for my bedroom.

Mother and Daddy separated a couple of years after I moved out, and soon Mom decided this house was much too large for her. She moved to an apartment. And I moved back home. Daddy coordinated the move so closely that one mover moved Mom out of Kenwood into an apartment and moved Michael and me out of the country and into Kenwood all in one day. Daddy said it was cheaper since it was considered one job.

I moved back to this house—but not to this room. I took Mom's old bedroom. The next thing I did was make my old bedroom into a dining room. The house already had a perfectly beautiful dining room: chandelier, bay windows, built-in china cabinet, chair rail on one side. The dining room is the room in a home you use the least; usually, it is reserved for eating and people and gaiety. I made this bedroom my dining room because I knew I would not have to spend much time here.

Still, I knew I had to deal with my sad memories of this room. Sometimes I sat in my newly christened dining room where my bed used to sit and examined my feelings to see if the room felt or looked the same. The view out the corner windows was the same, but the trees were larger and the woods out back seemed steeper than I remembered. (Perhaps the rumor about Kenwood Hill's moving is true! Houses on the hill show cracks in the walls as evidence of its shift.)

I recognized the black circular stain on the floor where the thirty-pound weight sat when it was not hanging from a rope along the ceiling with me on the other end, my head in a sling.

The aim had been to straighten my back. I was supposed to hang there for twenty minutes twice a day. How many days, months, years I don't remember—but from the looks of me, it was not enough.

When I first came back to this room, I felt the old oppression and loneliness. It has taken time, and growing, for me to be able to put those feelings where they belong. I balance them against the knowledge that I was pretty lucky. Still, I was a back-room person.

Several years later, after Daddy retired to his cottage at Lake Cumberland and Mom was in a nursing home, we tried to persuade her to come live here. We made this little room into a bedroom again, repainted it, carpeted it. But she would not leave the nursing home, maybe because she wanted the big bedroom or because this used to be her house. Or maybe because the nursing home felt like home to her. But, because she did not need this room, it became my office.

Actually, I avoid calling it an office, because "office" means "work," and I don't want to think of what I do in here as work. I call it the Kitty Room, because it was supposed to be my mother's room and her college friends called her Kitty.

I could have chosen another room as my office, but I chose this one to reclaim my memories and my history and to learn from what I had experienced. And to write about it. In 1982, in an article for *The Disability Rag* magazine, I wrote: "Unlike most minority groups, we do not have our own culture and traditions." I was wrong. But at the time, I thought of one's culture as one's background, one's mom and dad, one's grandparents. I saw culture as being where one came from. My ancestors were French, German, and English. My home, Louisville, has the Ohio River circling around, Churchill Downs, bourbon whisky, Olmstead parks—and these, too, are part of my background. I am proud of my heritage, my history, those things that formed us as a family, as part of an ethnic group. When I wrote that piece in *The Rag*, I did not see disability as related to my culture.

Since the majority of us with disabilities come from nondis-abled parents, we think we cannot connect to disability culture. Psychologist Carol Gill once said that people with disabilities are "cultural foster children." My parents taught me everything I needed to know about where I came from and where I was projected to go. But they had little experience with disability. The lessons I learned from my mom about disability were not accurate.

It's hard for us with disabilities to know who we are. Because others in our family have not had the experiences we're now hav-ing, we are, for the most part, alone. Not wanting to be alone, I believe, made me look for family at Warm Springs. I wanted to belong to Roosevelt's Warm Springs family, but I was born too late. Still, I found a part of it.

Like everyone, I was hungry for a hero. I found my hero at Warm Springs: Franklin D. Roosevelt. Some of my friends think I am obsessed with Warm Springs, but it is a big part of my child-hood and adolescence. I have learned a great deal about disability in America from Roosevelt and stories about him. It is a part of who I am; it is a part of my heritage, a part of my culture.

It was the belief that one must look to the past for lessons that sent me searching through my personal history. If I am to write the stories, I have to come back to the memories of this old bedroom. I have to come back to the pain and the isolation. I have to try and touch those memories, those events that made me who I am.

I've always thought that my experiences in life have been both diverse and universal. I know what oppression is, even though I come from a social class where there should be no oppression. I know what poverty is, and yet I come from an economic class where there should be no poverty.

From my experience, to grow up with a disability in Amer-ica is to live with unconventionality, confinement, and oppres-sion. We have to acknowledge that part of our culture has been oppressive—physically, economically, educationally, institutionally—an oppression often not acknowledged but real nevertheless.

It is sad that part of our past was painful, but it is a tragedy if we do not learn from it. That is why disability folks are coming together and getting involved. That is why we are chronicling and reclaiming our history, why we are teaching disability history, and why we are starting to write about it from our perspective. We are building a disability family, celebrating our culture.

"Skeptics notwithstanding, disability culture is incandescent and spreading," says Carol Gill. "I'm still betting on it to warm this tired world."[1]

This time by design, I am here in the room where I spent much of my childhood. This is not a big room. It's smaller still if it is your whole world. For too many years, it was my whole world. But I've come back partly because I expect the memories I find here to give me the energy to help define and celebrate our disability culture. The Kitty Room is a warm room now, a safe room and a safe place to remember.

Probably because I have spent so much time in here recently, I am comfortable. I enjoy it even when I remember the hard times. Sometimes the rituals of growing, the trials of moving from child to adolescent to "grown up," are not as important as the things we learn from those experiences. One grows because of them. Today, I feel I have the experience and the credentials and, finally, the credibility to do whatever I set out to do.

I am enthusiastic about being in the Kitty Room. I am encouraged by its accessibility; I feel quite capable now to take on any project. I have come back because this is *my* room.

1. Mary Johnson, "Emotion and Pride: The Search for a Disability Culture," *The Disability Rag*, January/February, 1987, 1.

2 True Home

Warm Springs

Tradition tells us that the Indian warriors bathed their wounds in the warm springs. A stricken warrior was granted passage through hostile territory if his destination was the warm springs. Thus the springs became not only a place of healing and rehabilitation but a place of friendship and peace. The Indians believed that a great and loving spirit living deep within the earth stoked the fires that kept the waters warm.
—*Roosevelt Warm Springs Institute: Information and Activities Book*

IN THE mid-Seventies, in the early days of my life as an activist, I got involved with a disability rights organization. Although I had really liked teaching freshman English part time at Jefferson Community College, I knew I wanted to concentrate my energy on disability issues. Most of my work was with Prime Movers, Inc. (PMI), "a research and consultation organization focusing on disability rights issues," as we said in our brochure. We wanted people to know that we were more than just a "crippled organization," and we hoped to educate and influence the prime movers in the community—the mayor, the county judge, media, funding sources, planning agencies—the decision makers. We wanted them to address the needs of people with disabilities in their community plans.

Prime Movers, Inc., was a small, all-volunteer nonprofit organization. We tackled what advocacy-oriented projects we could on our own, incurring as little expense as possible. We tried to educate public officials; we encouraged disability programming and community organizing; we worked with reporters—

The epigraph is from *Roosevelt Warm Springs Institute: Information and Activities Book*, a brochure by the Roosevelt Institute Volunteers, 1.

anything that might change public perceptions about people with disabilities.

In the early 1980s, I had the opportunity to travel to a national meeting in Houston, Texas, of the American Coalition of Citizens with Disabilities, the first national coalition of people with diverse disabilities. (My friend Mary Johnson and I had attended an ACCD board meeting in St. Louis in the early days, when the board still met in people's homes.) Although the Houston meeting would give me a chance to network, I was ambivalent about going. The more experience one gets, the more one is expected to do. By going to Houston I would put myself in a position to carry more responsibility. And I was not sure I could handle more responsibly right now.

On the other hand, I was feeling a new sense of confidence because of a recent PMI activity. For more than a year, we had tried to focus attention on how far behind Louisville was in building curb ramps on the corners of most downtown streets. We had gone to community meetings; we had met with city officials; we had written letters. Nothing happened.

So PMI staged a media event, the Great Wheelchair Race and Obstacle Derby, in late April, during the two-week celebration that precedes the running of the Kentucky Derby. Almost everyone in the city, along with most Kentuckians and former Kentuckians, celebrates during the Derby Festival, then watches the Kentucky Derby on the first Saturday in May. People who love horses, gambling, good bourbon, pretty women in hats, and Southern charm come to Louisville in May to celebrate. If they cannot be here, they have Derby parties and watch TV, wherever they are.

Because the Derby Festival is such a large, communitywide event, we were concerned about getting a permit and dealing with other legal issues. The Derby Festival officials, who could have prevented our race entirely, cautioned us only to make sure people knew the Great Wheelchair Race and Obstacle Derby was not an official festival event.

The Great Wheelchair Race and Obstacle Derby was a twelve-block wheelchair race through a heavy pedestrian area of downtown Louisville, including the blocks around city hall, the county courthouse, and the Hall of Justice. We planned it to include lots of obstacles, real and potential, like delivery packages and city garbage containers littering the sidewalks, broken curbs, and intersections without curb ramps. We had volunteers at each "obstacle" to make sure no racer got off course or cheated. We wanted to draw attention to the fact that, even though it had been years since a state law had required curbs ramps, the downtown was still inaccessible. Our wheelchair race was supposed to be unwinnable.

Of the ten racers, four used manual chairs and six used motorized chairs; we were surprised a motorized wheelchair made it into the fastest heat. What we did not anticipate was that two of our racers would be wheelchair jocks: one a basketball player, the other a wheelchair racer. They simply popped wheelies, hopped down the curbs, and finished the race. And we did not expect that a third racer, a prominent, refined law professor, would feel so macho, so competitive, that he would hop off an unramped curb in his motorized wheelchair and finish the race with a big smile and a broken axle. But the biggest surprise was Margaret, a sixtyish, gray-haired retired secretary, who ran the race in a rickety old manual wheelchair. By the time she finished the race, about twenty minutes after the jocks, most of the crowd had dispersed. Still, six of us couldn't finish the race because there were not enough curb ramps, the point we wanted to make.

When I noticed a newspaper reporter talking to Margaret, I was concerned. I didn't recognize Margaret from our meetings, where we had rehearsed what to say to the media. We knew how to explain the law simply, and we had background information to hand out. We were prepared to explain that curb ramps are not just for wheelchair users and don't hurt anyone. If reporters asked, "What about blind people? Aren't curb ramps dangerous for them?" we were prepared to explain the concept of textured curb ramps. We were not going to let reporters get off onto peripheral issues like disability rivalry or handicapped parking. And anyone who could not remember all the particulars could refer reporters to our selected spokespeople. I was one of those people.

I was in charge of media contacts that day, so I moved closer to Margaret and the reporter. He was interviewing her! He left before I could pull up beside her. "Congratulations! How great! You finished the race! I only got halfway around," I confided to her. "I had to stop. No curb ramps."

"We didn't think anyone could finish the race," I went on. "Well, maybe the jocks—but that's 'cause they're so athletic." My curiosity finally got the better of me. "How did you do it?"

"Well, like I told that young man," Margaret responded, pointing to the reporter, scribbling in his notebook as he walked away, "I did it because I had to."

Margaret told me that she used to work in an office downtown before she retired. She took cabs back and forth to work, but, once downtown, she was on her own. If she wanted to go shopping or to the doctor, she had to get around downtown on her own.

"But how did you actually do it?" I was intensely curious about her method. "Did you get out of the chair and take it down the curb and then get back in the chair? Or what?"

She explained that she would slowly back up to the curb, lean way forward in her chair, hold tightly to her big back wheels, and slowly let them roll down the curb. Then, with her front wheels still on the curb, she would slowly back away, until they too bounced off the sidewalk onto the street. Sometimes she had to travel all around the block looking for a curb that was not too high.

"The real tall sidewalks I can't do," she told me. "People notice and try to help. And sometimes I let them, if I know them or feel they can handle the wheelchair."

While she was talking, I was thinking. We had staged the whole event to show that wheelchair users could not get around downtown because there were no curb ramps. Yet this nonathletic woman was proving us wrong. I couldn't help wondering what she had said to the reporter.

"Well, yes, he did seem quite surprised that I was able to finish the race," she said, in response to my question. "But I simply told him that I didn't have a choice. That's the way it was in the past.

"But," she had told him, "it doesn't have to be that way anymore. Today we have a law."

I had never seen this lady at any disability meetings, but she taught me a lot that day. Her picture, crossing the finish line, was on the front page of the Metro section of the newspaper the next morning.

Dave Nakdimen, a local TV political reporter, contacted Mary Johnson for some follow-up and told her he was impressed with how well we had organized the event and surprised at how much media attention we had generated, considering it was Derby time. We made the six o'clock news and both newspapers—and the reporters, for the most part, got the story right. The event brought a positive response from city officials, who held public hearings, made a list of curbs to be ramped, and set timelines. It was progress. After all the positive feedback, I was hooked. That series of events inspired me to get more involved—so I decided to go to Houston.

As the sun rose, the countryside became more visible, more familiar. I looked out the van window. Railroad tracks on a ridge to my right paralleled the road, recalling years of traveling back and forth from Louisville to Warm Springs. The same railroad tracks, the same hills and dales and gullies and corners and curves and lines of trees. The same tracks I used to look for, all those years ago. And the same stomach ache. When I was little, my stomach would begin to hurt when I saw the tracks, for then there was no stopping. The tracks caught hold of me and brought me right into the tiny town of Warm Springs, Georgia.

Since we were headed south anyway, I had taken the opportunity to detour to Warm Springs and get my motorized wheelchair worked on. I lived there four times between the ages of nine and

fifteen, from four to six months each visit. In between, I traveled
with my family to Warm Springs every three to six months for
checkups until 1971.

This would be my first time in the town since childhood. I did
not know how I would feel, which I'm sure is why I waited to
come back with Michael and his sisters, Susan and Karen, people
who knew me as an adult. Coming back to Warm Springs as an
adult was important to me.

Michael was my friend, sometime boyfriend, and personal care
attendant. I have had personal attendants (companions, as I liked
to call them then) almost all my life. It is natural to me. Michael
and I were friends first. But my friends learn quickly that if they
want to spend much time with me they might be responsible for
providing a little personal assistance, like pouring coffee or helping me on with my coat. If they spend a lot of time with me, like
entire weekends, they can expect to do a lot more. Michael and I
had traveled together; he was used to me. About six years ago, he
lost his factory job (a bad placement for a musician!) and I found
myself rejecting my second prospective live-in attendant. I had
run out of prospects. Michael suggested we solve both problems
by him moving in with me and becoming my attendant. We have
been together now for almost five years.

When Michael's sisters moved to Louisville, they became my
little sisters. Now Susan and Karen were in their midteens (Susan was the oldest), and we thought it would be fun having them
along. Too, I was very ambivalent about this trip and thought the
girls might distract me from the emotional turmoil I expected
to feel about this return. We persuaded their mom, Gloria, that
the trip to Warm Springs would be educational for its history and
Houston for its lessons in citizen involvement.

In Warm Springs's earliest days, Indians believed that "a great
and loving spirit living deep within the earth stoked the fires
that kept the waters warm." When white settlers arrived, they
built cabins near the springs for their sick. In the nineteenth cen-
tury, Warm Springs became a fashionable resort, the Meriwether

Inn, which included a tavern, storehouse, confectionery, doctor's shop, blacksmith's shop, shoemaker's shop, and a dining room. Log cabins lodged visitors. Franklin D. Roosevelt stayed at the Meriwether when he first came to Warm Springs on the advice of a friend, George Foster Peabody, who had noticed improvement in people who had polio when they swam in the pools. In 1927 Roosevelt bought the property, 940 acres, and established the Georgia Warm Springs Foundation for rehabilitating people with infantile paralysis, as polio was then called.

At the age of nine, I knew only that Roosevelt had had polio and had come to Warm Springs. I found comfort in thinking of him here, and I wondered if he, like me, had felt apprehensive about coming back. If he had wanted to stop, to turn, to go back, like I did. I was almost sure he did not, because I knew he came back for vacations, whereas I came back for check-ups. If we had not done the exercises often enough, if I hadn't worn my corset and braces enough—if I was worse—then I would have to stay. Roosevelt was an adult at Warm Springs; I was a child when I stayed here and made him my hero.

So much of what I learned about Roosevelt came from people who knew him when he lived here. I heard stories of a man that the people at Warm Springs revered. All kinds of people. The meanest nurse's aide would smile broadly and change her mood instantly and dramatically when asked, "What was it like when President Roosevelt was here?" But he was also human. In the early years he lived with disabled people at Warm Springs, as one of them. He was getting "rehabbed" here, too. It meant something special to me to be where he had been. He felt like family, but for a long time I did not know why.

Whenever Michael and I traveled we drove at night. This time we had left home around midnight, and now it was dawn. How ironic: I'm in charge and I'm still coming back to Warm Springs at dawn. As a kid, I had hated arriving then.

My aversion to mornings probably started about four months after I entered St. Joseph's Hospital, when I was allowed to go home on the weekends. I would leave St. Joe's on Friday after-noons and go back on Monday mornings. In a way, that was a sensible arrangement, because my parents were not used to tak-ing care of a disabled kid and the aides at the hospital were. Daddy would take me back on his way to work and, to make sure he was not late, we had to get up really early.

When we started going to Warm Springs for my checkups, Daddy always insisted on early morning appointments. "The sooner we get your appointment the sooner we can get your x-rays, the sooner we'll get to the corset shop, the sooner we'll get to the brace shop, and the sooner we can get out of here and on the road home!" When I traveled to Warm Springs with my parents, we stayed at Fowler's Motel and went to the Foundation for my checkup. It was hard having to sleep in the same room with my parents. I didn't sleep much because Daddy snored loudly and I could not suck my thumb to help me sleep—my parents thought I had grown out of the habit years earlier.

I always had the earliest appointment, at 8:30 A.M. Usually, we would get up at the crack of dawn, get dressed, eat breakfast and get over to the Foundation by 8:15. If Daddy decided to eat breakfast at the Foundation, we would start earlier.

Now, almost twenty-five years since my first visit to Warm Springs, I am coming back at dawn. Suddenly the car stereo blasts out The Who's "Magic Bus." Michael knows the right music for the right occasion. I'm nervous but I smile, as Roger Daltry did on the bus. This is not like traveling with Mom and Dad at all.

The music wakes Susan up. "Hey, where are we?"

"See that railroad track?" I tell her. "That track will be beside us, beside this road, almost all the way there. When I was a little girl coming back to Warm Springs and saw that track, I knew we were almost there."

Since we had convinced Gloria that this was an educational trip, Susan had read up on FDR, so she knew these were the tracks that carried President Roosevelt back to Washington after he died.

She asked if I was excited when I saw them, excited to be coming back.

"I don't think 'excited' is the word," I responded. I was traveling with my mom and dad, I explained. I was living with them on the road, in motels, day and night for three or four days. It was too much togetherness. And Mom wasn't all that used to taking care of me. Chris, our maid, did most of my personal care at home. At Warm Springs Mom had to get me dressed and ready and get herself ready. The pressure of early morning appointments did not help. Besides, I told Susan, not knowing if I would have to stay was very disturbing. I did not mind the months I spent here—it was the coming and going that was hard. And, here I am, going again. "Actually, when I saw those tracks I would get a stomach ache."

"Well, we're here this time. And we'll have fun." Susan said.

A stir in the back of the van was followed by, "Aren't we there yet?" Karen was whimpering from inside her sleeping bag. Michael asked if she needed to stop, but she just moaned. "No, I just want outta this van!"

"Look! The Roosevelt Institute." Susan read the big white sign beside an unpaved gravel road. She was excited. "Turn in here!"

"Wait! Stop! Not here!" I said.

"What?" Michael shouted as he slowed the van. "Will you guys make up your minds? Where are we going?"

"It's the second road to the right. Not this one."

We turned in and traveled through tall pine woods until the road climbed a steep hill. At the top was a clearing with a small church and white houses and cottages to the left and many white buildings to the right. Susan pointed to a sign with the wheelchair symbol on it and the single word "crossing" underneath.

"How neat!" she said. "Betcha crippled people live here." Karen reprimanded her, reminding her that one was not supposed to use the word "crippled."

" 'Crippled' is okay," Susan insisted to her. " 'Crippled' is a word used among best friends. You're my friends, aren't you?"

Michael wanted the girls to settle down. He turned to me for directions. The road opened up into a large parking lot. I pointed to the Visitors/Out-Patient parking area. It was just as I remembered: white buildings, tall columns, black asphalt.

Michael and the girls hopped out of the van. He got my wheelchair, put me in it (on trips, I ride in the front seat). Susan and I went into Georgia Hall to register for our rooms while Karen followed to get a luggage cart. Back in the parking lot, we unloaded the van and headed for our rooms in Builders Hall single file, with me in the lead. Automatic doors swung open to greet us all along the way. "That's new," I remarked. Karen trailed me, moaning how tired she was and how this was supposed to be a vacation, so when were we going to have some fun? Michael followed with the luggage cart. Susan brought up the rear, hauling pillows and sleeping bags.

We had reserved two adjoining rooms in Builders Hall. When I was at Warm Springs as a child, this building was a dormitory where disabled people who could take care of themselves stayed. The long hall, with rooms on either side, looked like an old hotel with no amenities. I had never been down it before.

"This is it. Room 2." I passed the door and turned so Susan, with the keys, could open up.

"Let me!" Karen grabbed the keys from her and, after a little work, got the door unlocked and threw it open.

"Eyiii!" she shrieked as a large, black palmetto bug (which looked like a giant roach) ran out the opened door. I immediately put my wheelchair in reverse, Susan jumped out of the way, and Michael laughed. "Welcome to the South!" he said.

"I can't stay here!" screamed Karen. She refused to set foot in the room. "Come on," Susan said, passing Karen and falling on the closest bed. Another bug ran out from under the bed and Karen shrieked again. "I'm not staying here! I'm sleeping in the van!"

Michael told her she could sleep in the van if she wanted to, but she had to help him unload the luggage cart first; while unloading, he reminded her that she was a country girl and was used to bugs. Karen smiled weakly and started to help. She usually listened to her big brother and, after she saw the beds, she decided she was too tired to walk out to the van to sleep.

Once we got our stuff somewhat unpacked, we figured out the day. My doctor's appointment was not until one o'clock; I had insisted upon an afternoon appointment. All of us were hungry, so Susan and I set out to find food.

When we left Builders Hall, Susan asked, "Well, does it look any different?" One constant about coming back to the Warm Springs Foundation: Over the years it has gone through so many changes, you never knew what to expect.

Builders Hall looked the same but its use had changed. The cubbyhole near the entrance used to house a tiny gift shop. The whole area would be packed with kids in wheelchairs and on stretchers, trying to get snacks, comic books, plastic blow bubbles, and, sometimes, necessities like toothpaste or deodorant.

Georgia Hall had undergone the most dramatic changes. Built in 1933, it had been the core of the Foundation; the complex grew from there. Inside were the main registration desk, reception and recreation rooms, offices, and, at the far end, the dining room. In the main rooms, upholstered chairs clustered in groups around heavy wooden tables with tall floor lamps alongside them. Floor-to-ceiling windows lined most of the building's outer walls. You could tell how well the Foundation was doing by how Georgia Hall looked.

In its best times, it had a gentle Southern elegance and charm. But I had also been there when the Foundation fell on financially hard times. Then, the floors were torn up and the walls and ceilings peeling and badly in need of paint. It was scary to see such a grand hall look so shabby.

I was telling Susan about it all as we passed the front desk, when I noticed a large portrait hanging on the wall nearby. "They moved it." My voice was barely audible.

"What?" Susan had to double back. "Wow, that's neat! President Roosevelt, huh?" Susan recognized the unfinished portrait that Roosevelt was sitting for when he died.

When I was a kid, it hung in the dining room, behind the head table. People at the Foundation told stories about Thanksgiving when Roosevelt was here. He would greet people at the large glass double doors, the entrance to the dining room. Later he would sit at the head table and carve the turkey. He was like a grandfather to the children staying here. I could just imagine how neat that must have been!

"Hobnobbing with the president! But you'd be so old by now!" Susan giggled.

Things would have been easier for me, I told her. I think I could have understood and dealt with this disability life better if someone like him had been around to tell me how. I remember sitting in my wheelchair, feeling a strange sensation looking up at the unfinished portrait of this old and tired yet still strong man. A father figure. A person like me. Old man in a wheelchair; little girl in a wheelchair. I felt a connection to him. I felt pride because he was a great man and he was like me.

"Hey, let's go find food!" Susan begged. "I'm starving!"

We continued through Georgia Hall toward the dining room. My stomach was hurting. When my parents and I went to the dining room for breakfast, I would be so nervous before my appointment that I could not eat. If I saw kids I knew who had been my friends or roommates, I could not wave to them. I couldn't smile or even look at them. I had bad feelings I could not explain and never overcame. After my checkup—after I found out I was worse, or after Daddy fussed at Mom, or after I found out I didn't have to stay—I was ravenous. But beforehand, I could not eat anything.

I felt the same bad feelings now. Okay, I said to myself, this time I'm here with Susan, and thank goodness we have a mission: food. Still, I paused at the doors.

"Why did you stop?" Susan asked me.

In the old days, you waited at the door for the headwaiter, immaculately dressed in a black dinner coat, to show you to a table. Now when I peeked in the dining room it looked totally different. The room itself was the same, a long hall with floor-to-ceiling windows. Over the years, the windows had been covered with shades, or long, heavy drapes, or nothing. When I was a patient here, rows of tables lined the hall. Most sat four, but those farthest from the kitchen made up one long, head table, like the one Roosevelt sat behind for Thanksgiving dinner. Doctors and administrative staff sat there.

All of the tables then had white tablecloths and were set with silverware wrapped in cloth napkins; glass goblets were set out for water and iced tea. Black waiters in white jackets and dark pants served us all. The dining room with its soft-spoken elegance was nothing like a hospital, nothing like an institution. When I stayed at the Foundation, I felt privileged when I got to eat in the dining room. Not everyone did. You had to be old enough to know how to behave in a proper dining room. You had to be physically able to feed yourself. And you had to have enough "sit-up time"—the physical tolerance to sit up for three hours. When I was fourteen I got to go to the dining room only for dinner; my bones were still growing and my doctor was afraid sitting up too much would make my crooked back worse. When I was fifteen, I got to go for lunch and dinner.

Now, as I looked in, I was shocked. The tables were still there, but bare of tablecloths. Some tables were lined up in rows like high school; they looked as though they could seat twenty. To our right was the beginning of a C-shaped line drawn by stainless steel cafeteria steam tables, with neat rows of plastic trays, paper napkins, and Styrofoam cups at one end and mints and toothpicks and a cashier at the other. It was almost nine, and hardly anyone was still in the dining room. When we looked to see what food was left, we found cereal in boxes and milk in cartons, plastic bottles of orange juice and apple juice, some fruit, and—my favorite—doughnuts with chocolate icing.

We headed back through Georgia Hall to our rooms, my lap full of plastic utensils and a Styrofoam box of doughnuts, Susan carrying the rest. Before I got halfway down the hall I stopped in my tracks. Susan walked right into the back of my chair, bumping her shin.

"Ow! Whoa, Cass, sorry! What's the matter?" Then she saw what I had seen: an extremely handsome young black man in tight blue jeans and a short-sleeved red t-shirt that showed off his broad chest and well-developed arms. He was in a manual wheelchair and coming straight at us. "Hi." he smiled as he greeted us. His eyes were dark and mesmerizing, and he had long, thick, heavy dreadlocks. "How you been?" he said as he rolled passed us.

"Hi. Fine." Susan and I answered in unison. After he passed, Susan leaned over my shoulder and whispered excitedly, "He's gorgeous! Do you know him?"

I was in shock. "Yes, he's gorgeous," I responded, "but he's black!"

Susan understood the attraction but she couldn't understand the shock. "Cass, what do you mean? You're not prejudiced like that. He's gorgeous. No wonder you liked staying here."

How do you explain to a teenager in the Eighties what it was like in the South in the Fifties and Sixties? How do you explain that when Chris, our maid, used to travel to Georgia with us, she had to wear a nurse's uniform? Chris and I ate in the car when we were on the road because we could not take her in the restaurants. I told Chris I was glad we were eating in the car, because Daddy carried me into restaurants and sat me in a regular chair, and those chairs were so hard. I told Chris eating in the car was better; I was more comfortable there. When we stayed at Fowler's Motel at Warm Springs, Chris had to stay with Mrs. Fowler's maid, Ruby. Chris was a guest from a big city up north so Ruby would not let her use the outhouse; she brought Chris a chamber pot, and before Chris got out of bed the next morning, Ruby had cleaned the chamber pot and built a fire in the bedroom fireplace.

Now, in the early Eighties, how do I explain my shock at seeing a black patient in Georgia Hall? We always knew they were here somewhere, but Negroes had a special floor, a special treatment area. They did not get to go to the dining room for meals.

"Bummer," was Susan's response.

Back at our rooms, Michael and Karen were sound asleep, so we stashed the food in the cooler, Susan grabbed a banana, and we headed out again, back through Georgia Hall and outside into the courtyard. The sun shone brightly through the tall, thin pines. I was immediately hit by the familiar smell of pine, and all the good Warm Springs feelings came flooding back.

"Wow!" Susan exclaimed as she surveyed the campus. "This place is huge. And beautiful! Can I have a tour?"

I felt odd without one of my parents around. Everything was familiar, yet as I toured with Susan, I felt in some ways as if I were looking at the campus for the first time. The buildings formed a quadrangle. The yard in the center was parklike, with pine trees and bushes scattered about. All the buildings were connected by red brick walkways or porches.

Georgia Hall, behind us, faced south. To the immediate west was Kress Hall, which had provided overnight accommodations for family and visitors. When your family came to visit, you could check out of the Foundation and stay at Kress with them; it was like a small hotel. (You could also leave the campus altogether, but the city of Warm Springs was so small there was not much to do.)

Next to Kress along the quadrangle's west side was Founders Hall, built in 1957 for administrative offices, with classrooms for psychological and vocational testing. I had stayed at Warm Springs only once after 1957 and only once had gone into Founders Hall, probably for college prep tests. The open porch had the

Polio Hall of Fame exhibit. I showed Susan the bronze busts of people known for their work on polio, including Roosevelt, Salk, Sabin. "You sure can spout out the history of this place," Susan joked. "You sound like a brochure."

"Hey," I said, "I haven't told you any of the Indian stories. Should I stop?"

Susan laughed at me and shook her head no.

"You sort of learn this history in self-defense," I said. "It starts when you first tell people you have been to Warm Springs and their response is, 'Oh, yes, Hot Springs. That's in Arkansas, right?' 'No,' I would correct them, 'it's *Warm* Springs. Where Franklin D. Roosevelt went for the warm water and to the Little White House, his 'Camp David,' the place he'd come to when he needed to get away from Washington.' "

Often people would insist I was wrong, which amazed me—until I realized they thought I was just a kid and thus could not possibly know.

"Should I stop?" I asked Susan again.

"No! I was just kidding," Susan responded. "You don't sound like a brochure. This is kinda fun. I like knowing what you did as a kid."

The Wilson Building was next. In the early days, it had been the infirmary. People stayed there for a few days to be evaluated when they first arrived at Warm Springs. I found this out when my teacher at home suggested I read a book about a girl my age who also went to Warm Springs. Since the heroine had stayed there between Roosevelt's and my time, I found the book very appealing. It made things more real, because the heroine's experiences reinforced mine. It also made me realize that, even though I had missed Roosevelt's era, I had been at Warm Springs at a good time in its history.

When I stayed at the Foundation, the Wilson Building housed the pool, a physical therapy area with tables and curtains around each, and an area with whirlpools. I was disappointed to learn early on that FDR never swam in the Wilson pool, built in the early 1940s. It was easier to take the water up the hill using pumps than to take the patients to the old swimming pool down the hill that FDR had used.

"What's that?" Susan pointed. Far down the hill in front of us was the walking court. It was a place to exercise, to practice walking up and down steps. Susan wanted to take a closer look.

Sitting at the top of the long, steep hill, I realized I had never gone down it by myself before. This was the first time I had traveled the campus without someone pushing my wheelchair. At this hill, whoever was pushing would assure me, "Don't worry, we won't go fast." Nonetheless, I had been terrified. Even though I wore a seat belt, I could see myself toppling out of the chair—the hill was that steep.

Now, an adult in a motorized wheelchair, I could go wherever I wanted and as slow or fast as I wanted. My wheelchair has gears, so it could not run away with me. Still, I couldn't get out of my head those memories of teenage boys racing down this hill in their wheelchairs joking and shouting, "Runaway chair! Get outta the way!" I asked Susan to walk behind me holding on to the handles of my wheelchair—just in case.

We headed to the walking court where, in more populated times, people spent hours strengthening their muscles on exercise steps in one corner and parallel bars in another. I had never used them, since I never did any walking. I loved that walking court, though, because in the summers, the recreation director cooked hot dogs and marshmallows down there. All the kids on the medical wing would be on the balcony in wheelchairs or propped up on pillows on stretchers. Patiently waiting for our food, we fed the squirrels, blew soap bubbles (or, better still, plastic blow bubbles), or played cards. This was hardly like being in the hospital at all. It was more like summer camp with exercises and physical therapy.

That was Roosevelt's idea, too. He understood that even institutionalized young people needed social interaction. So he made sure young people from the local high schools and the local girls' college worked at Warm Springs as recreation directors, assistant physical therapists, and pushboys. "Pushboys" were young men hired to push us all over campus. During "work hours," they pushed us to and from therapy, the pool, or the brace shop; after hours, it was to the dining hall, the movie theater, or wherever we might wish to go. That was how Roosevelt got around. It made immense sense to me.

One day a pushboy named Freddy was taking me from Third Floor East to the gift shop at Georgia Hall. All we had to do was go down the hall, out the door onto the porch, across the arcade and then to Georgia Hall. But instead, Freddy took me in the other direction to the elevator. When I started to say something, he stopped me by saying. "I'm going to take you a special way."

When we got in the elevator, he pushed "Down," and the elevator went down and opened on a dark hall painted in rich, soothing colors on a floor I had never seen before.. To one side was a sitting area with big armchairs and a table similar to the ones in Georgia Hall. I was a little jealous because my floor was not so nice.

Freddy knew where we were. He told me he meant to take this detour and he kissed me on the lips quickly. Then the elevator closed and we were on our way back upstairs to Georgia Hall. I found out later that the basement floor was where the black patients stayed. Susan giggled when I told her about the kiss. "No wonder you liked staying here!"

The balcony on Medical was fun but being on Medical itself was not. Medical was like a real hospital. You stayed there if you were going to have surgery or plaster casts put on to straighten your legs or back, a process made possible by wedging. Usually done once a week, wedging involved cutting the cast halfway around from front to back, opening it a crack, putting in a wooden wedge, and then wrapping the wedge in with wet plaster. The goal was to shift the spine—first to one side, then the other—until the back was straight, or at least straighter.

A girl named Cindy used to come to Warm Springs in the summer and get a short body cast from under her arms to her knees. She would stay a few weeks, get all wedged up, and go back home to Texas in the body cast. There were no wheelchairs for people in body casts, so her dad carried her everywhere. Her family must have really loved her to go to all that trouble.

I stayed on Medical twice: in 1957 for a body cast to straighten my back, and in 1959 for surgery. "God, you stayed here a lot." Susan said.

"Well, I was a kid. Disabled kids grow, change, need new braces. And when you go for a check-up and you're worse . . ."

In 1959, I had surgery on my left hip and leg and wore long leg casts to straighten my knees (wedging again)—all so I could stand. Not walk, mind you, just stand. When the doctor decided to do the surgery, he cautioned my parents and me: "Now once we do the surgery, you must do your exercises and wear your leg braces so you don't undo the benefits." I needed the surgery precisely because I had not done the exercises enough or worn my braces enough. At age fourteen, I decided that sometimes doctors were not too bright.

After the surgery I was taught to stand with braces and crutches—just stand and balance. It was good for me, the doctors said. For me simply to stand meant going through this procedure: getting get the braces on, getting them locked, being pulled up out of my wheelchair into a standing position, positioning the crutches, and leaning me on them. In this tripod position, I was to balance. Balance! Propped on crutches I could not hold onto, crutches I was attached to with wrist straps and elbow straps. They stayed under me only because I was leaning on them with my weight, standing with braces locked at the knees so I did not crumple to the floor. I could not lift my legs to move my feet, to step, to walk. I had no muscle power for that. So I stood there, twice a day, five days a week, for about twenty minutes.

I was not alone. We had standing classes in the Functional Department every weekday right before lunch—half a dozen to a dozen people, all kinds of wheelchairs, braces, crutches, all degrees of disability. Some people actually walked in standing class. I just stood there, balancing and thinking: How do I learn how to walk? How far could I go if I did? How fast could I get there? What would I feel like once I got there? What would have I accomplished?

I concluded that I would have worn myself out and scared myself half to death—standing was very scary to me. I soon realized walking was not what it was cracked up to be. In a wheelchair I could get so much farther so much faster, and I did not even have to push myself! What was the point of walking? Where was it going to get me? How would it make me a better person? At fourteen, I decided that walking did not serve me any good purpose; for me, it was no longer a goal.

By now Susan was bored with imagining parallel bars, pretending to walk between them. "Come over here," I called, as I headed toward the arcade in front of Medical. "I need to get out of the sun for a while."

"Cool, birds!" Susan had spotted the solarium below with big brass bird silhouettes mounted on the roof, part of the Children's Pavilion. Once the polio population decreased, Warm Springs started treating people with disabilities like strokes and spinal-cord injuries. When children became the minority, the Foundation built this wing just for kids. I had never stayed in the Children's Pavilion; by the time it was built, I was too old. I was kind of envious of the solarium, although I thought its huge cage filled with dozens of live Java birds and parakeets a bit extravagant.

Dr. Haak, my doctor at Warm Springs, often blustered about how the metal birds on the roof were a waste of money, even if they reflected the donor's sense of art. Dr. Haak thought the money should have been used for braces for children who couldn't afford them. This taught me my first lesson in charitable giving:

The most important thing is that *donors* feel good about what they have done.

Next along the arcade was the East Wing. Most of the time when I stayed at Warm Springs, I lived there on the third floor. I thought East Wing Third was the cool place to be, perhaps because the first time I came here to stay, I stayed on Second. When after a few weeks, they moved me to Third, my nine-year-old mind may have seen the move as a sign of progress.

And all the neatest, best-looking people lived on Third. I did not think of myself as a cool person. I knew I was on Third because all of Dr. Haak's patients stayed there. Sometimes I'd become fearful that someone would realize I wasn't cool and make me move.

The people who lived on Second just weren't cool. They were like kids from a different school or another neighborhood. They looked different, they didn't dress as nicely, they weren't as attractive, they didn't act cool. It had nothing to do with economics, or education, or disability. I think it had to do with community and belonging. Ironically, I found out years later that Janet, my best friend from college, had stayed on Second when she was a kid. She was probably there around the same time I was, but because she lived on Second, we would never have been friends.

By now Susan and I had walked almost three-fourths of the rectangle made by the buildings and arcades. Susan was beginning to feel the lack of sleep from riding in the car all night, so we headed back up the hill. Halfway up, she recognized the brick courtyard outside Roosevelt Hall. "That's it! That's the place you had your picture taken with President Kennedy!"

She ran up the hill, across the arcade, and into the all-brick courtyard. On either side of big picture windows were bas-relief sculptures, "symbols of rehabilitation," each with a quote inscribed beneath. One sculpture depicted FDR sitting in his chair with a large cape around him; beside him stands a child with braces and crutches. His quote read: "There is nothing to fear but fear itself," which I always revered even though I was not sure I understood what it meant. The other bas-relief showed Helen Keller and her teacher Anne Sullivan. Helen Keller's quote said: "They said it couldn't be done but it was done." During the JFK photo shoot someone had outlined the quotes in white chalk so they could be easily seen.

The photo of me with John F. Kennedy has always had a nice place in my homes—never conspicuous, not on a mantle or dresser, but usually tucked on a bookshelf among my other memorabilia. No one can visit my house for long without noticing. "Is that . . . President Kennedy?" they ask. "Why, yes," I reply nonchalantly. And then I explain.

Every Democratic politician who vied for the presidency after the death of Franklin Roosevelt went to his Little White House at Warm Springs, Georgia, during their campaign. There was great excitement when it was announced that John Kennedy was coming. He would be speaking at the Little White House but could not come to the Foundation to "greet the patients," as FDR had; his schedule was just too tight. So the Foundation was asked to send some patients over for this photo op. I don't remember how they made the final selection but it seemed like almost everyone wanted to go. Once I learned we had to get up at six A.M. to get over to the Little White House in time, I took myself out of the running.

The night before Kennedy's arrival, those going to the Little White House had to go to bed early. Since two of my roommates were going, we all had to turn in early. I guess because of all the to-do, I griped: "What's the big deal? He's just a man."

The next morning the food carts rolled onto the floor an hour early so the "chosen ones" could eat before their trip to the Little White House. By the time I got breakfast, my scrambled eggs were cold and my milk and orange juice were warm.

The only thing I hate worse than mornings is anything that messes up my morning routine. After years of hating breakfast, I had learned to enjoy it at Warm Springs. Even though I was usually on a low-calorie diet when I stayed there, breakfast was one meal a diet did not destroy. So I was upset all over again.

I was fifteen years old. My sister's boyfriend was Catholic, so there had been discussion in my home about the country having a Catholic president. I was not political, but I knew that when it was time to register, I would choose the Democratic Party; my grandfather always said, "If you want to have a say in politics here in Kentucky, register Democrat." But voting was several years away. Upset about my ruined breakfast, I decided, then and there, never to vote for John Kennedy.

I ranted to anyone who would listen. During one of my tirades, the head nurse came running down the hall shouting: "He's coming! He's coming to Georgia Hall! Senator Kennedy is on his way over here! He's squeezing us in! If you want to see him, we'll take you up there! Hurry up, if you want to see him!"

As she ran past my room, Joe, one of the orderlies, popped his head in my door. "You want up?"

"No!"

Since I had griped about his visit, I couldn't become star struck now. Before I could say anything else, Joe had pulled a stretcher from the hall, propped pillows under one end of the mattress, and lifted me out of my bed and onto it "You want to see this man," he insisted. "Someday he might be president—and you can tell your grandchildren you saw a president!"

Joe was going to make sure I did not miss this opportunity. I was on the stretcher and out the door.

The hall of Third East was crowded, but outside was worse. The front porch on Third was huge, large enough for a dozen people in wheelchairs or on stretchers to congregate there in the evenings and on weekends when families came to visit. Now it was so packed with people that I could not see across it.

I had been at Warm Springs during the celebration of the twentieth anniversary of the March of Dimes. For a whole week, the *Today Show* and *Queen for a Day* broadcast from the campus.

Now, as I was being wheeled on a stretcher through the crowd, I realized this event was even bigger than that!

All of a sudden, a voice hollered: "Stop! Bring her over here!" Someone grabbed the stretcher away from Joe and pushed me into the courtyard outside Roosevelt Hall.

"Right here," said Susan now. "I recognized it in your picture." She was standing where I had sat that bright and shining day I met John F. Kennedy. Being semi-reclined on a stretcher facing the sky probably enhanced the effect. A gaggle of photographers and reporters rushed toward me and hollered: "Over here, Senator Kennedy! Look over here! Come over here!"

And, all of a sudden, there he was! He came through the crowd right up to *me*! He took my hand, said hello, and started talking to me. The sun was bright on his face. His hair seemed auburn, but the sun made it golden; his eyelashes were so thick and long, I could hardly see his eyes. I don't know how he saw through them. He was very nice and very handsome. All around us was a commotion of people swarming, badgering, begging: "Please, Senator, look over here!"

He finally looked up at them and said firmly: "Excuse me. I'm trying to listen to her." And he turned his back on them!

After all my fussing and complaining, I was in my hometown newspaper the next morning in a photo with the future president of the United States. Mom got the original photo from the newspaper and had it framed for me.

By now Susan was peering into Roosevelt Hall's lobby windows. "There's furniture in there. It looks kinda old-fashioned. Can we go in?" I said we would have to go to the theater door around the corner from the courtyard. There we were greeted by two huge metal doors that seemed to intimidate Susan. I told her it was the regular route to the Functional Department. Usually the doors were propped open, for although Roosevelt Hall was state-of-the-art access when it was built in the mid-Fifties, it did not have automatic doors.

The auditorium, a lobby, and a sitting area were on this floor.

The Functional Therapy Department, the Occupational Therapy Department, offices, and a small brace shop were downstairs. In the lobby, Susan got a better look at what she termed "old- fashioned" furniture. Actually it was 1960s style. This lobby, like Georgia Hall, was always a good indicator of how well the Foundation was doing financially. It had to be presentable because it was a showplace for many of the important events. Now in front of the fireplace sat two avocado-and-orange striped couches, four yuck-green plastic upholstered chairs, and two skinny-legged end tables.

I told Susan I did not want to go downstairs to the Functional Department. I had never liked visitors coming around when I was in Occupational Therapy or standing class, although I didn't mind being a part of show-and-tell for a special occasion. I was once filmed working with the head of the Functional Department, trying several designs of hand braces until we found the one that made feeding myself easier. We worked on it four days; he even filmed us working together. I liked that kind of attention.

Functional was neat also because it had a complete wheelchair-accessible apartment where people were taught to adapt to living at home. I didn't get to do all that—I did not have enough muscle function. But seeing the apartment with all its adaptations helped me realize I could live a regular life.

I liked the OT department because there they let me do the things I could. Perhaps that is a bit of an exaggeration: When I made brownies, I did grease the pan, but I couldn't wash my hand off by myself; when I designed and printed up a box of Christmas cards for my grandmother, I placed the type in the printing press, but I couldn't tighten it. When I typed letters home to my mom or Maw-Maw on the electric typewriter, someone else put the paper in for me.

Susan wanted to see the theater. We had to get past another set of wide metal doors to enter the auditorium. When they swung closed behind us, it was dark and quiet and kind of spooky until our eyes adjusted to the dimness. The open area before us divided into curved hallways. As Susan headed toward the first one. I told her to wait: that hallway took people to theater seats, and I didn't fit there. Susan followed me down the farthest, darkest hall, which finally opened into theater.

Inside was a stage with dark blue velvet curtains and a huge movie screen. It looked like any other movie theater, except the three rows closest to the stage were empty.

"Where are the seats?" Susan asked.

"I'm in mine," I told her as I positioned myself in the first row, facing the stage. Susan squatted beside me as I recounted some of my experiences in this now-dark theater. I had seen a stage production of *The Importance of Being Ernest* when I was twelve, feeling special because the kids I knew back home had never been to a real stage play. Popular local and national entertainers performed for us here. There were first-run movies on Thursday and Saturday nights for those of us twelve and older and on Saturday afternoons for the kids. (I seldom got to go to movies at home.) Not only the people who worked and lived on campus but people from all over the Warm Springs area came to the movies here.

I saw racial segregation in this theater, too, I told Susan. When I was at Warm Springs segregation was the norm. I knew black people did not get to do everything white people got to do—there were no black nurses or therapists. And I knew there was something wrong with calling a white aide an "aide" and a black aide a "maid." But discord among the races was not obvious on campus.

Until a gathering.

One evening I was propped up on a stretcher in the auditorium, waiting for a movie to start. The lights had begun to go down when a commotion erupted on the far side of the auditorium—whispering and laughter and the thumping sound made by people folding down the theater seats. I twisted my neck to look behind me, which was hard lying on the stretcher, but there seemed to be so many people—and they were all late! I had to see what was going on.

My eyes were just beginning to adjust to the darkness; everything looked shadowy. I finally saw them in that far back corner of the auditorium: maids, orderlies, waiters, janitors—and their families—coming into the theater from the far entrance after everyone else was settled. As was the custom of the day, as I told Susan, the Negroes could not be seated until after the white people were in their seats. She finally understood why I had been shocked to see dreadlocks in Georgia Hall.

"Let's go back to the room," I suggested. Susan was tired and slightly spooked. As we headed toward what in my days would have been considered "the colored people's" door, I said, "I've never been out these doors before."

Back at Builders Hall, I knew I could not sleep, and I wouldn't be happy sitting around a room while others slept. I had been energized by the Grand Tour. So I made sure Susan was settled and went back out onto the campus. This time, I headed down the hill by myself, terrified still but knowing I could handle it— as long as I did not stop before I reached the bottom of the hill. A quick stop would throw me forward. My seat belt would keep me from falling out of the chair but at best, I would be embarrassed; at worst, I would fall forward and not be able to right myself.

From the bottom of the hill I crossed over to the Infirmary, past the pool, and out of the quadrangle. I followed the sidewalks that passed the brace shop, the laundry, the schoolhouse.

When I stayed at Warm Springs, I never had enough sit up time to go to the classrooms, and I had never been in the schoolhouse. I usually had school in my room, between nap time and OT.

I came upon the new Georgia Department of Vocational Rehabilitation building. Although one approached it by a long covered walkway, it was definitely not as stately as the buildings of the quadrangle. This modern, red-brick building shouted "government facility"—but it seemed welcoming nonetheless, so I rolled up to the front door. It was automatic. I love automatic doors. I do not have to sit around trying to look nonchalant while waiting for someone to come along so I can say: "Excuse me. Would you mind?"

I went through the automatic door at this new-to-me building. It was lunch time by now, so hardly anyone was around. I wandered the halls in my chair. I noticed that they were wide and that the doors were, too. The doors had levered handles. So accessible. So cool.

I read all the bulletin boards, again trying to look like I belonged here. And then I saw it. A water fountain at the other end of this long hall. It attracted my attention right away. It was shiny, bright chrome. It was beautiful. It hung out from the wall about chest high on me; no pedestal, nothing underneath it; I could roll right up to it. I had never used one on my own.

When I was a little kid, when I could walk, I needed someone to lift me up to a water fountain. After I got polio I could never reach one from my wheelchair. Now I just sat and looked at it. I timidly went toward it. I could get right up to it; my foot petals went right underneath it. I could reach the handle; I could push it down. I could get a drink of water by myself. I was in ecstasy! And embarrassed that I was giddy at the thought of drinking from a water fountain.

I looked around. I did not want a witness if I dribbled water down my front. I found it takes practice. I quickly learned that the water bubbled in an arc and I had to lean over far enough so dribbles didn't go down my chin. After a few tries, I was able turn the water on and off at just the right time so I didn't get too wet. I felt so accomplished. Here I was at Warm Springs, in my thirties, feeling accomplished because I used a water fountain by myself. I felt welcome here.

By now it was 12:30. Even though my appointment was not until 1 o'clock, I left the VR building and went straight to the Outpatient Dept. in Kress Hall. It won't hurt to be early, I thought to myself. Dr. Haak was no longer there. That was no problem, though, since I was just going for wheelchair repair—tires, batteries. I did not need a check-up. I just needed a doctor's authorization to get the work done. Still, I felt strange. In the past coming here for check-ups was traumatic. Now, coming back as an adult,

I kept having a nagging concern that someone might say: we have to keep her this time.

"Does her back look worse?" Mom, Daddy, and I would all look at the x-rays when the technician brought them into the examining room. The examination rooms were always huge with an exam table in one corner, two or three chairs in another, a huge, institutional metal desk with a desk chair with wheels and padded arm rests in another corner, and on the wall, above and to the right of the desk, hung the back lit x-ray screens. The room was so huge there was room for all of this plus my wheelchair. There was plenty of room to stand with braces and crutches and walk, if you could, so the doctor could check the condition of your braces, to see if the leather needed replacing, or if you had outgrown them. Since I didn't walk, I didn't have to do that. Thank goodness—because I could not imagine my mom trying to stand me up by herself. Daddy never did that sort of thing at home, so he would have been no help.

"Yes, the curve in her back is worse," Daddy would answer his own question. "Haven't been wearing your head traction, Cass. Mom, not doing those stretching exercises enough. Dr. Haak is going to fuss at us. I have to work all day, to make a living so we can pay the bills, pay for these trips. You all are going to have to do better." Why, I wondered, did he always blame Mom? She would look so helpless. She could not take care of me by herself. She had Chris to do housework and help take care of me, including the exercises, but it was still too much. It was not anyone's fault.

You're not twelve years old anymore, I kept thinking to myself as I entered Kress Hall. You're not twelve or fourteen, you're not with your mom and dad and your not going to have to stay.

I knew when I made my appointment several months ago that Dr. Haak was no longer at Warm Springs. They gave me an appointment with Dr. Hoffman; she did not work at the Foundation full-time so there were only certain days I could schedule with her. She was the first female doctor I ever had, so I was curious to meet her. As I passed through the automatic door at Kress Hall, I could not help being sad that I never had a motorized chair when I stayed here before—I would have had way more fun!

"May I help you?" The lady behind the registration desk asked. Her thick, slow Georgia accent reassured me and calmed my nervousness. I apologized for being early and mumbled something about getting in early, getting out early and on the road. I signed myself in. The lady behind the desk helped me get my insurance card out and fill out the papers. The Foundation was always a place where you did not have to do everything for yourself. Here it was natural to have assistance.

Since I was early she asked me to wait in the waiting room. This incarnation of Kress Hall as the Outpatient Department was a great improvement. It had carpeted floors, upholstered high back chairs, cherry end tables; I am sure it was institutional furniture but it was expensive furniture. Kress Hall also had floor to ceiling windows; the windows opened into the courtyard between Kress and Builders Hall. As I looked across the courtyard at Builders, I tried figure out which rooms were ours (where Michael and Karen and Susan were, hopefully, sound asleep). Nope, I am not here with Mom and Daddy this time. I'm here on my own. How bizarre!

Soon the receptionist called me from the hall. She showed me into a small office with a desk, file cabinets and bookshelf but no exam table, no x-ray screens. There was just enough room for me and my chair. I think it was the first time I had ever met a doctor in an office rather than an exam room.

Dr. Hoffman came in and we had a few minutes of small talk about her being my first female doctor, about her working part time at Warm Springs and working for other hospitals. She knew Dr. Haak, had worked with him. She confirmed that he had had heart problems and was not doing too well. I did not want to know more. Sometimes you do not want to hear the facts.

But, I was not surprised. He and Daddy used to talk sports and fishing, but you could tell Dr. Haak was not athletic. Dr. Haak was tall like my dad but he was built like my grandfather: with a big stomach. In my teens I was told, "Don't get fat because it will be hard for others to take care of you," so I was perpetually on a diet. When the years passed and Dr. Haak started talking about his having to diet, I was secretly glad.

Dr. Haak looked like Paw-Paw but his hair was black. He smelled like my dad and my granddad—Old Spice. Doctors can be scary, but if they smell like my dad, I'm not afraid of them. He smoked cigars like my dad—only he smoked them all the time; my dad smoked cigars only on special occasions. I loved the smell of cigars.

When I went for check-ups, he would come in the exam room, greet us all, shake hands with Daddy, sit at his desk chair and look at my folder. Then he would roll his chair over to the x-ray screens, talk about whether my back looked the same or was worse. He would roll over to me lying on the exam table, all the while talking about me and what the x-rays revealed. He'd take my hand and say, "Well, Princess, how are things going?" He called all the little girls "princess." I knew I wasn't the only one, but I felt special anyway. He would check my hand splints and leg braces to see if they needed adjusting or repair. His voice was deep and strong (like my dad's) and when he fussed at us for not doing my exercises and wearing my braces enough, he always had a look of sympathy on his face that told me he did not believe it was my fault.

During our talk about Dr. Haak, Dr. Hoffman leafed through a thick folder that must have held years of medical records. As she sorted through the papers, I noticed a familiar yellow legal-paper handwritten letter. I had written to Dr. Haak several times over the years when I wanted to talk to him without my parents around—once when I had an experimental hand brace that was awkward and ugly and I was going to high school and I did not want to seem so different. And once when I began dating.

I was in college at the time and I wore a hard, plastic back brace. It was shaped like me only a little straighter; it was made from a plaster mold of my body; it covered my hips and went to my bust. One day at a pool party at Janet's parents' house, I met a nice young man. We were sitting in Janet's kitchen, talking (I was in my wheelchair so there was no deception there) when he put his arm around my waist. I wasn't soft! He tapped on the brace— but before he could ask, Janet jumped in, "She's a plastic fantastic lover!"

As soon as I got home I got out my legal pad (I always write better on lined paper) and frantically wrote, "Dear Dr. Haak, I'm beginning to date and . . ."

At my next check-up, Dr. Haak rolled over to me lying on the exam table and said quietly, so only I could hear, "Try to find a firm foundation garment. You can substitute it for the back brace on special occasions." I really liked Dr. Haak.

Dr. Hoffman was nice, too. She looked like a school teacher with glasses and her hair up in a twist. She did not wear a white jacket and was so easy to talk to that she really did not seem like a doctor. We talked about the condition of my wheelchair and, since Medicare needs authorization for everything, she wrote up an order for the brace shop to give my wheelchair a once-over and to supply me with new batteries, new tires and whatever else was necessary to keep my chair in good working condition. She would send an order to the brace shop; the paperwork would take a few hours to complete. I liked the brace shop a lot now that I did not go there for braces. The brace shop was actually the orthonics department; they did everything, brace making, hand-splint making, shoe fitting and channels for braces, crutch adjustment, wheelchair fitting and maintenance. The shop was pretty busy, she cautioned; they might not be able to get to me today. "That's O.K.," I said without thinking. "We planned to be here two days."

I left Kress and headed back to Georgia Hall. For a moment I wondered if I should go get Susan before I headed out. But I realized I liked being here alone. So again I headed out on my own at the Georgia Warm Springs Foundation.

I looked out past the Georgia Hall parking lot toward the cottages and the dirt road winding between them. Some of the cottages were small, others were two-story houses, but all were made of wood and painted white. And they all had ramps or flat entrances. In the early days, families of patients built cottages at the Foundation and in the surrounding woods. Some people lived there year 'round; some came for vacations or stayed the summer. Others were built for doctors, therapists and staff.

I decided to take this "road less traveled." I realized I had never been off the quadrangle on my own before. No one had ever wanted to push me that far in my manual wheelchair.

As I started out I wondered if my motorized wheelchair could make the climb. We had been driving all night and had not had a chance to charge the batteries. If I got stuck, though, I reasoned, Susan would come looking for me—eventually.

As I explored this new area of the Warm Springs campus, I found myself looking closely at the houses that had been home to the therapists, doctors, and nurses I had known here. One of them, McCarthy Cottage, had been home for Roosevelt before the Little White House was built. I knew I was far out when I passed this one.

I used to think that when I grew up I would come back and live here. I remember deciding that if I found the real world too hard a place to live in, if I found it too hard to get a job, to live with normal people, then I would come back and live here.

I was past the cottages when I noticed, at the end of the road, a circle of grass, meticulously manicured, and beyond it the edge of an emerging thick, pine woods. I stopped my chair. Something had caught my eye—something that looked like a very short person. I moved closer and saw that it was a stone bust. Out here, alone, at the end of the road, away from the cottages, was a bust of Franklin Delano Roosevelt! "You're everywhere around here," I said aloud as I approached the face carved in stone.

"Are you talking to me?" I heard a voice behind me, startling me. I turned and saw Susan standing there with a paper plate with two huge chocolate doughnuts on it. "Shit, I forgot the napkins!

I guess we'll just have to lick our fingers. Who were you talking to?"

Susan finally noticed the sculpture. "God, he's everywhere! The Father of All Crippled People," Susan said. She popped a piece of chocolate doughnut into her mouth and offered me a bite.

I motioned it away. How different it felt to be here without parents, I told her. How good it felt to be back—but also how strange. Susan asked me if I ever thought I'd walk again. I reminded her that I had been disabled a long time. Chances for recovery become slim after a couple of years, I told her.

I was nine years old when I got polio. I knew I was very sick for awhile, I was in an iron lung. I nearly died. But I thought I would get well. When I got over being infectious, I was moved from a private room into a ward. All kinds of kids were in the room—some of the parents were very upset that kids who had polio were put in with their kids. One mom, I remember, came to our defense. She was small, had dark hair and her baby was in the hospital in an oxygen tent. She said something about being properly educated about this disease and that everyone knows that once the temperature was down, a child was no longer infectious. I liked her right away.

And I helped her, too. I was a light sleeper and one night I woke up because I missed the hissing sound of the baby's oxygen tent. I became alarmed and put on my signal light. The tank had run out of oxygen. I saved the baby's life! His mom was so happy she spent time with me and helped me cross-stitch the alphabet. I could not really poke the needle through, so she would do that, then hook the thread around my finger and let me pull the tread through.

I did think I would get well. I thought I was getting better. I went into the hospital in August; around Christmas they began letting me go home on weekends and special occasions. In February, they let me go home for real.

I had been home just a few weeks when my sister said to me—she was just a couple of years older—"If I were you, I'd be walking by now. You must not be trying." I remember sitting there and thinking to myself, OK, how do you do that? What do you do? Sit there and say, "Move, muscles! Move, muscles!"? That doesn't work. I tried that. Nobody tells their muscles to move and they move. It just happens. How can you learn that process?

When you are a kid you do not know what "getting well" means. You don't know how to do it. You don't know what's expected of you. You don't have choices about exercise and therapy and eating right. You do what they tell you to do.

"Getting well" or "being cured" is more complicated than that. It can mean many different things. By the time I got polio in the 1950s, "cure" in almost everybody's mind meant only one thing: to eradicate the disease. To preserve normalcy. But for me, even then, it meant something different than that. I remember lying in bed at night when I was little, trying to go to sleep, uncomfortable, having to go to the bathroom, or needing a drink of water or a blanket, and not wanting to call Mom. Not wanting to hear her moan, "Oh no! Oh, my, I have to get up?!" Not wanting to hear Daddy awakened, startled, and snap, "What's the matter? What is it?"

So I would not call. Instead, I would try to occupy my mind so I would not think about needing to go to the bathroom. I had gone to Sunday school enough to have some idea that miracles sometimes did happen. If you prayed. So when I was awake trying not to call Mom, sometimes I'd pray. Except for me, being a child, it was more like making a wish. Did I wish to be cured? In my fashion. But usually my wishing would cause me to fall asleep, and then I would dream. In the dream there would be an angel. The angel would tell me I could have one wish. I would ask to not have had polio—that was expected, of course. But, as I knew would happen, the angel would tell me, " That's too big a wish. You can't have that. Ask for something smaller."

I told her I wanted to walk. Again she'd respond, "You can't have that. That's too big a wish, too." I thought about the kids I knew at Warm Springs who didn't walk. They did O.K. To me, walking was no longer that important. If I could just get around by myself, that would be OK. I saw kids at Warm Springs getting around fine in their wheelchairs, pushing themselves—they were cool.

I would ask for a straight back, good arms and good breathing. If you had those you could handle yourself, get yourself around, dress yourself. You could get yourself to the restroom when you needed. That was the most important thing. But then the angel would tell me that was "too big a wish," also. The straight back would quickly become expendable. (I knew people with crooked backs who got around O.K.) Until, finally, my wish was scaled back to "just arms. If I can just have good arms I could dress self, get in and out of my chair, I could go to the bathroom on my own." Then I would wake from my dream and still had to go to the potty or was still cold. Nothing had changed.

Roosevelt was not looking for cure when he came to Warm Springs. It was treatment—which he explained meant making people's lives better—that was really uppermost in his mind. For Roosevelt, the goal of treatment was to make people as productive as they could be. He developed exercises and braces, and his ideas influenced rehab thinking all over the world.

Neither Roosevelt nor those who worked there ever claimed that people got cured at Warm Springs. What did happen at Warm Springs, though, was more important than cure. Roosevelt lived with disabled people at the Foundation as one of us. He was getting rehabbed too. He experienced peer support before the term had been coined.

"You know," Susan said, "living here, when you were a kid, it must have been really neat. Lots of kids your age. You guys could get around on your own. Not like having your Mom drive you to church or school, or the movies. You must have been real happy here." Susan offered me a doughnut. I shook my head no.

"Are you ever going to eat?"

I wasn't really listening. I looked at the statue again. I kept thinking, *home*. Was it "home" to me? I was happy when I stayed here. The kids I lived with here were different like me: they all wore braces, used crutches, had wheelchairs. They were like brothers and sisters, like family. I realize now that being at Warm Springs was important to me because I was with my own kind here. They did not stare at me—because they looked like me. They did not ask me ignorant questions because they knew the answers.

But I found it traumatic to switch back and forth from being a disabled person among disabled people, as I was at Warm Springs, to being a disabled person all alone, as I was when I came back home to Louisville. When I remember the times I was unafraid and unalone as a child, I find that those were the times I was at Warm Springs, Georgia. It is a paradox to think an institution can be liberating, but for me it was. I was not confined there as I was when I was home.

I learned about life with a disability and how to get along in the world—life lessons. My family had little experience with disability; they could not teach me those lessons. When my parents came to visit, I sometimes felt as though I didn't belong to them. I was someone different, someone from Warm Springs. When they came to take me home, my parents seemed like strangers. I did not belong to them.

Strangers called this place a hospital, an institution, assuming (and making me feel) that I could not be happy here far away from home. I would get a stomach ache when my parents came to take me home and when I returned with my parents for check-ups. On visits to the Foundation, I could never bring myself to speak to the other children I saw there. I know now it was because I came back with my mom and dad and they were the strangers. *They* didn't belong.

When I was with Mom and Dad, I felt like I did not belong either. "I should have been happy here." I said out loud. "But people kept taking it away from me."

3   Attendant Vibrations

One night, FDR's son John returned to the White House late and noticed that his father's light was still on. Going into the presidential bedroom, he found Roosevelt in his chair. The president had rung repeatedly for his valet, Irvin McDuffie, for help to go to bed. McDuffie, who liked his drink, had had too much, fallen asleep, and had not responded to the bell. FDR was stranded, unable to care for himself.
—Hugh Gallagher, *FDR's Splendid Deception*

THE FIRST time I read this passage, I was stunned. I stopped, went back, and read it again: Roosevelt "was stranded, unable to care for himself." Understanding Roosevelt's disability as I did, I would have thought he could get himself into bed. "Just give me arms," I used to pray. I knew Roosevelt was strong. Whenever you saw him, in whatever kind of picture, he looked strong.

I looked at Roosevelt as a role model, and I wanted to see him realistically, but I was shocked to learn that he needed so much assistance. Perhaps the bed was just too high. He got help, though—exactly what he needed to live the life he wanted: ramps, car controls, walkers, valets. And so did I, sort of. The similarities between his life and mine were beginning to overwhelm me.

I was sitting up, late at night, just like Roosevelt. I was not stranded, but I had been, many times. Tonight I was staying with Claudette—a friend and attendant—for the weekend, sleeping in her back bedroom. My regular attendant (which Roosevelt's valet was, of course) hadn't gotten drunk and fallen asleep; I had given him three days off—something I felt obliged to do periodically,

The epigraph is from Hugh Gregory Gallagher, *FDR's Splendid Deception*, rev. ed. (Arlington, Va.: Vandemere Press, 1994), 115.

since the state program that gave me funds to pay him did not give me enough funds to pay him adequately. Our solution was that occasionally I would stay with friends and Michael would get two or three days off.

"Stranded, unable to care for himself." Franklin Delano Roosevelt, the leader of the free world, I learned, had to have attendants every day of his life after he became disabled. He was lucky to be rich enough to afford them. But he also got assistance because people thought he was worth it. Whatever he did was important enough that he would have what he needed.

Sitting in Claudette's back bedroom, I realized that I was lucky, too. I've had a regular life because of attendants. I could not have had a life without them. If I had even more assistance, I could do more. If I had lots of assistance, I could be president too—if I wanted. (But I don't!)

You know how sometimes you meet just the right person at just the right time? For me, Claudette was one of those people. I met her over the phone when I was taking information-and-referral phone calls for the Center for Accessible Living. Like most grassroots nonprofit organizations, the Center was underfunded and understaffed. So, as Center board members, Jewell, Sharon, and I had volunteered to come in three afternoons a week to take care of those calls.

The Center for Accessible Living started with the dream of a few people, who asked, What do we really need? What would be the best solution for the disability problem? It is exciting to realize that disability folks in communities all over the country were asking the same questions and coming up with the same answers. The Center for Accessible Living, Inc., was the result. Louisville's Center opened in January 1981 as a housing program funded by the city. The organization helped people with disabilities find and adapt housing, taught them how to deal with housing discrimination, and provided technical assistance to builders and housing providers. In October 1981, a $200,000 grant from the U.S. Department of Education allowed us to become a full-fledged independent living center, which meant we provided services in housing information, employment, peer counseling, personal attendant care services, and self-advocacy to people with disabilities.

As I&R phone volunteers, Jewell, Sharon, and I returned calls to people asking for information about the Center or other disability resources, a job the staff would have done if they weren't so busy. We felt valuable because we were doing the same job— and, sometimes, we did it better. Often, because of our own life experiences, we were able to help people who called—which is what independent living centers are all about. We had the time, since we did not have paying jobs, to volunteer for this work, and it was rewarding.

The Center gave us a spare wheelchair-accessible desk, since all three of us used motorized wheelchairs; they gave us a phone, supplies, and a resource Rolodex. We shared the desk: Sharon used the drawers on the left side; I used the ones on the right. Jewell didn't have any drawers, but she couldn't open them anyway. Sharon and I had to make sure that the Rolodex sat on the front right corner of the desk so Jewell could reach it. Once we made our shared work area accessible for all three of us, we found the job was not too hard.

The day I took the call from Claudette, she said she was new to Louisville, had been involved with disabled people and independent living programs in college, and wanted to hook up with one. She told me she had been an attendant at her university, and she wanted to know what was going on in Louisville with attendant services. I was happily surprised to find someone who understood the concept.

She had never lived in Louisville before but had visited her aunt here often, and now that her aunt had died—and left her a house— Claudette was going to settle here for awhile. In school, she had been in charge of coordinating students and schedules for a program that matched college students with people who needed personal attendants. She told me about a wheelchair-using professor who not only had attendants come to his home to bathe, dress, and get him in his wheelchair, but also had someone come to his house in the afternoons and take him out to a bookstore nearby for coffee and readings.

We talked often over the next couple of weeks. The program Claudette had worked for was the kind I was looking for. I wanted to ask her more about it, but I was afraid I would learn that it was not as wonderful as it sounded—that it was a pilot program, or only for professors. It was on a college campus, so I was sure it did not reflect the real world—or could not be replicated in the real world.

Still, talking to her I got excited about the possibilities. Disability folks in Kentucky were gearing up to go back to our legislators to increase the budget of our state personal attendant care program. I told Claudette about our effort: how we began with half a dozen volunteers, disabled and nondisabled, who did research and organized people all over the state and then got legislators to put a bill before the general assembly. We were basically asking the state to provide money for disabled people to hire personal attendants, people like Chris or Michael or Claudette.

To get this accomplished, in 1984 we had people with disabilities from all over the state going to our capitol in Frankfort three days a week—during January, February, and March, the worst months to travel in Kentucky. I was renting a house in the country at a landscape nursery in Lyndon, Kentucky. To get to the front of the property, where the van taking me to Frankfort would meet me, I had to drive my motorized wheelchair a quarter of a mile on a gravel road from our house.

The March day our bill was to be voted on, there was already snow on the ground at 8:30 in the morning. I was used to being in all kinds of weather, but this blowing snow was a bit extreme. Michael was so concerned about my trip down our road to the van that he followed me in our car in case I got stuck.

Why didn't he just drive me? In those days Michael and I had a Chevette; I know it seems absurd for someone with a motorized wheelchair to own a Chevette, but it was inexpensive and we were paying for this one ourselves. Usually, Michael just took the wheelchair battery off, collapsed the chair, put them both in the back of the car, and off we'd go. But all that would have taken too much time this morning, so he followed me instead.

I was afraid of the snow, but I had been one of the "cheerleaders" in this lobbying effort. I was proud of what we were trying to do. I had talked it up with people I knew, and they were all going (although they didn't have a snow-covered gravel road to travel). Now I knew what our grandparents meant when they said, "We trudged five miles in the snow to school. . . ."

During that legislative session, disabled people attended committee meetings. We wore buttons. It was hard not to notice us: two wheelchairs in a meeting room, we soon learned, looks like a crowd! We encouraged disabled folks who couldn't come to Frankfort to call or write their legislators and have their friends call and write—and their spouses, boyfriends, cousins, and anyone who knew them and could understand the value of personal attendants.

The Kentucky General Assembly funded the new personal care attendant program during a session in which they were trying to cut programs. I think they funded us because we so overwhelmed them. One legislator said, "I couldn't go back home without this program—my constituents wouldn't let me." That year, they gave us a small pilot program to serve one hundred people. It was not much, but it was a start. And we were grateful—with thousands of people with disabilities in Kentucky, we were grateful that a hundred of us had a chance for a regular life.

When I met Claudette, I couldn't help thinking, Here's a warm body, a new person—I hope I can get her more involved. But after I talked to her, I realized she would not be comfortable talking to legislators, and she really wasn't interested in driving people to Frankfort. Since I was looking for more help myself, Claudette came to work for me two times a week.

She didn't need to work. She had savings and money from her family to fix up her aunt's house, and income from the house's second-floor apartment. Her fiancé, Dave, a pastry chef, arrived from Ireland and was immediately offered a job at a very fine downtown hotel. He had a wonderful Irish accent, and he was very nice to look at and comfortable to be around. Claudette was an earth goddess in wool sweaters, long dark skirts, socks and sandals. She wore her great thick auburn hair in a Dutch-boy cut. As I got to know her, I realized that Claudette really liked being a personal attendant.

I had been excited about coming to Claudette's for the weekend. She and Dave were now married, and she often took their new son, Luke, on walks. I would have the opportunity, after ten years away, to boogie around the Cherokee Triangle, my old neighborhood, on my own. The Cherokee Triangle was named for triangle-shaped Cherokee Park, one of the original parks designed by the great landscape architect Frederick Law Olmsted. Like Iroquois Park near my house, Cherokee provided a peaceful setting in the Triangle neighborhood.

The area was developed in the late 1800s by businessmen who guessed that people were ready to move away from the river. To get from the neighborhood to town, the residents had to be affluent enough to have transportation—horses—and their homes were stately and large. Because of the income and status of many residents, carriage houses, stables, and servants' quarters were common. Soon a trolley line helped create business along Bardstown Road, and grocery stores, bakeries, pubs, and services sprang up.

After World War II, many affluent families, in Louisville as elsewhere, left the city for the suburbs. By the time I lived in the Cherokee Triangle in the mid-Seventies, large homes that had once housed three-generation families had been converted into apartments (rent due weekly) and upscale carriage-house apartments. A well-manicured yard full of flowers might sit next to an unkempt yard full of uncut grass and weeds.

This was where all my friends wanted to live when we were finally able to afford our own places. Jerry, a young college English teacher, was the first of my friends to move there. We met during my second year of college (his first), but we did not get to know each other right away. He was part of an intellectual, sophisticated Oxford-cloth-shirt group. I hung around the periphery of that group—but one of the great things about my college was that it was so small there wasn't really a periphery.

When I began my apartment search five years after graduation, Jerry offered to help me. By then he and I were often considered a couple. (In those days many people in my group were pairing up but not necessarily committed. Once when we both were recovering from bad relationships Jerry and I pledged that if we didn't find anyone better in ten years, we would marry each other.)

As was the custom, Jerry biked around the neighborhood looking for rent signs until he found 928 Cherokee Road. It was close to Cave Hill Cemetery, the part of the Cherokee Triangle closest to town, and the least expensive place to live in that neighborhood. It was two doors from a florist shop; a pizza distribution store shared the alley.

The neighborhood by then housed professors and students, young career people, doctors, nurses, and starving and affluent artists. Wealthy professionals moved there because it was one of the nicest old neighborhoods. My dad always wanted a house in the area because he grew up thinking rich people lived there. Many of the poorer people worked in the businesses along Bardstown Road and lived on the side streets. The Cherokee Triangle had become, and continues to be, an economically diverse neighborhood.

Jerry knocked on the front door of 928 and met the landlady, Mrs. Hagemann, who showed him the apartment. I'm sure he laid it on thick about how responsible I was, and about how I had my family to back me up financially. When he called me with the news that he had found me a large, *affordable* place to live *on* Cherokee Road, he was excited.

I called Mrs. Hagemann immediately to make sure it had not been rented already—things go that fast in that neighborhood—and I made an appointmentt. Other friends, Sandy and her husband, Tom, took me to see the apartment.

Of course it was not accessible, so Tom took me in my wheelchair up the front steps and through one of the two front doors: one had opened into the entry hall in the original home, but Mrs. Hagemann had converted the entry hall years ago into a small apartment for herself. I later learned there were two other apartments on the second floor and one attic apartment.

As soon as we came through the front door, I was sold. The entrance had tall windows on each side and a leaded-glass transom above the front door. The first-floor apartment was everything I could have hoped for. The living room was huge, with a twelve-foot ceiling, a fireplace (nonworking), and a mantel. The second room had probably been a formal dining room; it had a large ornate chandelier and tall windows that looked out onto the bare walls of the house next door. It was almost as large as the living room, and I chose it for my bedroom. There was a tiny kitchen (which looked more like a hall), a dining room, a bath, and a second bedroom in back next to the bathroom.

Modern apartments were cracker boxes with a living room, dinette area, kitchen, and two bedrooms side by side. Most could fit into the first two rooms of this place! Here the two bedrooms were separated by three rooms—essential for the privacy of an almost thirty year old living "on her own" for the first time

Mrs. Hagemann and I hit it off right away. (Jerry warned me that once I signed a lease, she might stop being so nice.) She would let my dad build a ramp to the back-door entrance, which was not required of landlords in those days.

Daddy and a friend built the ramp over the back steps. To save money they did not build a landing at the top, which meant that when I came home, someone had to go up and open the back door and then come down and push me up the ramp and into the apartment. I did not have a motorized wheelchair in those days.

* * *

Claudette's Cherokee Triangle duplex had no built-in ramp, although I could get around once I was inside. The bathroom was not accessible, but I brought portable facilities so I didn't need to get in there. A nice little back room served as a spare bedroom. I bought a hospital bed from Goodwill for $50. The bed raised and lowered so it was easier for Claudette to get me in and out. Michael moved the bed to Claudette's the same day he checked the place out to see the best way for me to get into the house.

"It'll be okay," he told me. "We've had worse!" That was not comforting, I told him. It was not meant to be, he replied with a smile. There were steps from the street to the front yard, and more steps from the yard to the porch—so forget the front entrance. There were steps to the back door as well, but I had portable ramps that could get me up them.

My ramps were aluminum troughs, one for each side of my chair, with rubber strips so the tires could grip to prevent slipping. Each was four feet long when folded but opened up to eight feet. Even with handles for carrying, they were very heavy, so Michael had decided to set them up himself.

In preparation for my weekend at Claudette's, I packed clothes in my purple cloth bag; it hung easily on the wheelchair handles on the back of my chair. I took my little red-and-blue suitcase with my potty (bedpan) and toiletries inside. I also hung my leather pouch on the back, filled with work (board and staff reports and personnel policies to review), magazines, and a brand new copy of Hugh Gallagher's *FDR's Splendid Deception*.

I took a TARClift bus, a small bus with a wheelchair lift. TARClift was the public bus service for people with disabilities. The bus came right to my door and took me straight to Claudette's—but I had to schedule my ride two weeks ahead of time. I asked the driver to drop me off in the alley behind the house, but it was too narrow for the midsize bus to turn into. So the driver let me out at the alley entrance. We stopped traffic. In this old neighborhood with its narrow side streets, that was not unusual.

Luckily, Claudette was watching for me and saw the bus circle around, so she and Luke, in his stroller, met me in the alley and helped me carry my stuff. The alley, the parking area, and the back entrance into the yard were rough with loose gravel and broken bricks, but Michael was right: I was used to this kind of terrain. Michael and I used to plow through fields, pine forests, and gravel roads when we lived in the country. I considered myself pretty macho when it came to wheelchair travel.

I had felt confident about going to Claudette's because we had the portable ramps. But when I saw the ramps propped on the many steps to the kitchen door, my heart skipped a beat. Architectural regulations say ramps should be twelve inches in length for every inch in height; if you have a step three inches high, you need a three-foot ramp. Claudette's house had ten steps; it was maybe thirty inches up to the back porch, so the ramp should have been about thirty feet long. My ramps were eight feet long, nowhere near the proper access ratio, and very, very steep.

Suddenly my backyard journey seemed almost insurmountable.

To make matters worse, my ramps could be wobbly. If they were not lined up just right, my wheels would not roll up them. A wheel could pop off one side, leaving me dangling. If I was going into Claudette's house, she was going to have to get behind and push with all her strength to get me up that steep incline.

"Let's go in. I want to show you around!" Claudette was excited. I begged off.

"I just got here. Let's stay outdoors for a while." I had decided that I would go in and out of the house infrequently and, while outdoors, I'd pray for no rain, so we would not have to run for cover.

Claudette took my stuff in and came right back out. It was a bright, sunny day. She had done the laundry, so we talked while she hung it on the clothesline. When she was done she started to go in with the laundry basket, leaving Luke on a blanket on the ground.

"Wait! Where are you going?" I had heard the phone but I was startled that she hadn't grabbed up Luke and taken him with her.

"You can watch him," she called back as she raced into the house. "He can't walk or crawl yet. He can't get away from you!"

I was sitting in my wheelchair; he was on a blanket at my feet. I could envision him rolling all the way across the backyard and right out into the alley.

I am not a kid person. I have never wanted children myself. Well, maybe when I was little I did—but after I became disabled, I realized I was not going to be able to bring up a kid without a nursemaid or nanny to help, so I reasoned that unless I was rich and could afford the help, I would not have children. I didn't mind. I didn't feel a loss.

But I got annoyed when people patted me on the shoulder and said: "What a good attitude you have. Of course you don't want children, since you can't have them, can you? You shouldn't have children anyway, because it would be such a burden for others!" That angered me because it sounded as though I had not made the decision to remain childless of my own free will—the well-thought-out, reasoned, and seriously pondered decision it had been.

I also felt that if I could not devote eighteen years of my life to a child, I shouldn't have children. And I knew I did not want to devote my life to anyone else. I figured I would have a hard enough time taking care of myself. Besides, my sister, Ann, had four kids and, since we both believed in zero population growth, she said that she had had mine. Ironically, when she said that, it was the only time I felt pain about not having children. Even though I was adamant about not having them, for that one second, I felt a loss—as if someone had taken something from me.

I was a good aunt, though. I got to know Ann's kids pretty well. Once I had my own apartment, they came to spend the night. I did not experience all the baby stuff like diapers and vomit, but those visits were enough to satisfy me.

Now I was sitting in Claudette's backyard, watching a baby that was not supposed to move much roll himself over from his back to his tummy. I couldn't believe it.

"Claudette," I called out. "Claudette! He's moving!" Luke looked up at me from the blanket and giggled. Just before Claudette came out of the house, Luke flipped himself over onto his back again.

"Claudette. He turned over!"

"He can't turn himself over yet," she protested. "He's too young,"

"He did. I saw him!"

"No! How?" Claudette was laughing at me.

"Don't ask me how," I told her. "I haven't turned myself over since I was nine. He just did it.

"Look! He's doing it again!"

Thankfully, Luke turned over again, in front of us. I was mesmerized. How easy it seemed! He just put his foot put down on the blanket and pushed down on his heel. That made his butt go up off the blanket and he turned and rolled over—so easily!

So that's how you do it. Luke did not learn to do it—he just did it! Here was information I wish I had known that day at Warm Springs in the Functional Department when the therapist said, "Let's put you on the mat and see what you can do." I had thought they would ask me if I could turn myself over, and my reply would be no, and that should be that. But no.

Come to think about it, the therapist told me to do exactly what Luke did. She even bent my knee up with my foot on the mat. She told me to push down, which I tried to do, but nothing happened. She pushed on my knee to push my heel down and make my butt go up and said, "Try again." Still nothing happened. My heel and knee hurt from the pressure, but my butt did not go up in the air. I did not turn over. She could demonstrate the movement but she could not "teach" me to move. She could not teach me how to make my muscles work. I always expected physical therapy to hurt, but going through the mat episode to prove how incapable I was seemed demeaning. I felt abused.

Now, since it was almost dinner time at Claudette's, I knew I could not avoid those ramps any longer. Just as I feared, it was scary. The ramps needed lining up; Claudette had to prop the kitchen door open so I could go up the ramp, onto the porch, and up the one more step into the kitchen without—if possible—stopping. She had to walk up the steps between the ramps as she pushed my chair, and I worried she might stumble. But I prayed, she pushed hard, and we got up and inside the house.

Dave was working late that night, so Claudette, Luke, and I had the evening to ourselves. I sat at the kitchen table while Claudette fixed dinner, then got in bed early, set up so I could work and read in bed, so Claudette could spend time with Dave after he got home.

I decided to stay in bed the second day at Claudette's. Dave had the day off and slept late, and Claudette was able to get me pottied, dressed, and presentable before he woke up. It was also easier for Claudette if I stayed in bed. She had a baby and needed to do housework. But we planned to spend my last day walking through the Cherokee neighborhood.

So I was in bed in the back bedroom, ensconced with folders, magazines, and *FDR's Splendid Deception*. I reviewed the Center's newly revised personnel policies as well as I could. (Jewell was always better at personnel issues than I was. I was better at writing grants and developing programs.) I was tired of working, and I wanted to do something fun. So I started looking at *FDR's Splendid Deception*.

There he was in the photos. Franklin Delano Roosevelt. My hero. At Warm Springs, in Washington, D.C., walking, not walking. I wanted to read the book fast so I would have all the answers, yet I realized I didn't know all the questions yet.

I read chapter 5 first, because it was about Warm Springs. Next I read chapter 1, "Onset." As I read, I kept thinking: Tell me something I can say to people that will help them understand about the disability situation.

I had thought the same thing when I read *The Feminine Mystique* five years earlier: Please, tell me something I can use to help people see that "the plight of the disabled" is societal in origin— our problems are not because we cannot be cured. That book helped me realize that, like women, disabled people also have "a problem with no name," that people with disabilities should not buy society's view of who we are. Just as women are not the weaker sex, disabled people are not less than human.

Gallagher's book was the first to really investigate the disability Roosevelt had due to polio. All other FDR books romanticized the polio as an "episode": He got sick, he got well, he became president. I think Gallagher drew some wrong conclusions about President Roosevelt, but he provided more physiological information than I had about my own disability.

Within the pages of *FDR's Splendid Deception*, I discovered the extent of Roosevelt's disability. He hid the fact that he could not walk, but it was natural for him to have a valet to help him to bed. I am sure Roosevelt's son never contemplated putting the president in a "home" because he couldn't get in bed by himself. The idea was ludicrous, but it helped me see how differently "personal assistance" was viewed when it was for a very powerful person.

When we were organizing to get the state attendant care program passed in the legislature, one of my jobs was to go to a couple of nursing homes and visit residents who were young and with the proper resources would be able to live outside a nursing home. I was to encourage them to work for "the cause." During these visits I met Bill. He was thirty-five, an ex-army guy who went into a nursing home because his wife had to work and could not stay home and take care of him. He was a quadriplegic from a spinal cord injury; he needed a lot of assistance and there was no state money to pay attendants.

I felt uneasy during the entire visit. I knew a nursing home might be in my future as well—we all know that.

During my visit an aide came in. "Bill, are you going to get up in your wheelchair today?" she asked him. "If you want to, you'll have to get up right now, 'cause I'm going to the other end of the hall and might not be back down this way today."

I had only twenty minutes until my ride picked me up, so Bill told her no and continued to talk to me. I felt bad that he missed what may have been his only opportunity that day to get up in his chair.

Bill shared his room with an old, thin man who appeared to be comatose. Putting them in the same room probably made sense to the nursing home: They needed the same "level of care." If Roosevelt's son had decided that his father could not care for himself, would he have put him in a nursing home? What would his roommate have been like?

Now, sitting in Claudette's back room, an intense feeling of sadness for this great man overwhelmed me. I had been stranded many times, and it had always seemed just one of those things. But when I read that Roosevelt was stranded, I felt indignant. How could anyone treat the president of the United States this way? When I thought about how I felt when I had to depend on someone else to accomplish a basic task and had no one there, the old feelings surfaced. The embarrassment I felt at being seen as "incapable" now extended to Roosevelt. I was embarrassed for him.

I felt connected to Roosevelt. We were all connected, all of us who need personal assistance to live our lives. The job of getting someone undressed and into bed is no different, whether the disabled person is the president of the United States, me, or my friend Bill. It was the perception that was different.

Looked at realistically, everybody needs assistance. We have personal assistance to be born; we will have assistance when we die. Personal assistance comes from moms and dads and teachers or classmates. They are drivers at $5 an hour, or chauffeurs at $75 an hour. They are people who type your reports, file your papers, prepare coffee for your business meetings. The only real difference between the secretary fixing coffee for a business meeting and my attendant fixing coffee for my friends is their respective wages—and society's perception. The difference points up the deep problem with our attitude toward personal assistance services for people with disabilities.

Personal assistance traditionally has been the family's responsibility. That is why it was never a problem for Franklin Roosevelt and people like him. He could afford it and was used to it, long before he became disabled. People who were well off had assistance. A woman expected her "lady's maid" to help her with dressing and bathing. A man got help from a valet with shaving and dressing. This was a concept Roosevelt was familiar with.

Although I did not think we were rich when I was growing up, I have had attendants almost all my life. I became used to it, too. My first experiences with personal attendants came in the hospital when I was nine. After I had polio I stayed in the hospital until February, although I came home for weekends and holidays. At home, my assistance came from Mom and Daddy, my big sister, my little brother, and anybody else who was around and offered to help.

Once when Daddy did not get home for dinner, our next-door neighbor carried me to the bathroom because Mom wasn't able. I was embarrassed, but Mom said: "He has a daughter. It's not like he hasn't seen a naked bottom before." But he had not seen mine!

In 1955, when I came home from rehabilitation at Warm Springs, I was ten years old. I had been out of school for a year, but I had classes at Warm Springs, so I kept up with my Louisville classmates and when I came back, I was able to attend half days in fifth grade with them. The elementary school was new and accessible, which in those days meant all on one floor. Of course there was a step from the parking lot onto the sidewalk, and each classroom had a door to the outside with a step. But I was little, so it was not that hard to take me and my wheelchair outside.

At home, my mom was my personal assistant: She had to bathe

me, dress me, get me in and out of the car. She was also my driver. My body was not strong enough for me to spend a whole day in school. After lunch, my mom would come get me. At school, I never went to the restroom, because it would have taken too much personal assistance. (Twenty-five years later when my friend, Mary Johnson, ranted and raved against inaccessible restrooms, I said, "To make a restroom accessible to me, Mary, it would have to have a bed in it!")

I had personal attendants at school, my classmates. Each Friday, my teacher would decide which girls would be my assistants for the next week—two, in case one got sick and so one could stay in the hall with me while the other went to the bathroom. They helped me with my books and pushed me back and forth to the lunchroom and playground. One of the things Warm Springs did for me was teach me to know what assistance I needed, and how to instruct people to properly assist me.

One day I noticed a couple of boys talking to the teacher right before she made her weekly announcement. "Danny and Billy asked me why I always pick girls," she told the class. "Didn't I think boys could do the job? they asked. So I'm assigning Billy and Danny to be Cassie's helpers next week. That's all right with you, isn't it, dear?"

One of the boys was cute and I had a big crush on him. It would bother me to have him as an assistant—but not in a bad way. The other boy was nice looking too, and I liked him because one of the first things he said to me when I came back to school was that even though I had braces and a wheelchair, I was still cute. I was *still* cute? I never knew he thought I was cute!

Then I got concerned: How was I going to feel sitting outside the boys' restroom door? How embarrassing! How awkward! But at the same time, how flattering that Billy and Danny wanted to assist me. I was shocked that boys would want to be helpful. What was I to say? I blushed and said yes, it was all right with me.

That December, I went back to Warm Springs. Dr. Haak said: "You've been sitting up too much. Your back is worse. If you go back to school, you can only sit in your wheelchair for an hour at a time. The rest of the time you must use a chaise longue and not sit any straighter than a forty-five-degree angle."

At the age of ten, I made one of the worst decisions of my life. It was important to me how I looked. I used a wheelchair; I wore short leg braces and brown high-top shoes; I had metal hand braces and a canvas corset to keep my back straight. (Of course, the corset was under my clothes and could not be seen, but I felt self-conscious anyway.) Going to school in my wheelchair and having someone pick me up out of my chair and sit me on a chaise longue during classes, then get me back in my wheelchair to go to lunch or outside for recreation just seemed like being too different.

And who would do it? Mom had two other children at home to care for. She could not be at school all morning. This was long before the Individuals with Disabilities Education Act, which provides aides to kids in school. There were no laws assuring an equal, accessible education for children with disabilities.

So I told my parents I could not go to school. It was probably best for my mom, since she was having a hard time with all the responsibilities. My not going to regular school would make everything easier for her. None of us realized that I was isolating myself. By staying in school I would have been staying in the real world. Someone, an adult, perhaps, should have realized that my staying home was not the best solution.

I was twelve when Chris came to work for us. She had worked in a factory, but she had a new baby and she wanted to be home more. Her job was to clean the house, do laundry, and help Mom take care of me. Chris was my first true personal attendant. She was two years older than my mom. Besides bathing me, dressing me, and washing my hair, sometimes she got me out of bed and into my wheelchair. She took care of me in a way my mother could not.

On weekends, when Chris was off, the personal care I got was haphazard at best. Mom found it easier if I stayed in my pajamas on the weekends, and if I used the bedpan only once a day. I did not grumble: It was one thing I could do to make things easier on my mom.

Sometimes when Chris returned on Monday morning, she found me soiled or wet. She seemed upset while she cleaned me, but she could never bring herself to say anything to the family about it. I did not understand at the time that she needed the job and she worried about what would happen to me if she were no longer around. I never admitted to Chris that, to make things easier, I often did not tell Mom when I needed a potty.

It did not seem strange to have someone taking care of me. After all, I was a little kid: Kids don't take care of themselves. Sometimes I pretended to be a character in a novel, someone going on a ship to England with her paid companion. I liked the word "companion." That's the way I liked to think of Chris. I went through stages when I made her wear a white uniform so it would look like we were rich enough to afford a nurse. Later, I made her wear colored uniforms because white looked too medical. "Made," perhaps, is too strong a word. I was twelve years old. I could not *make* Chris do anything.

In fact I knew that, to have a life, I needed the assistance of others.

When I was allowed to go to high school, I decided Chris should wear regular clothes again—I did not want to seem different. Daddy did insist, though, that she wear a nurse's uniform when she traveled to Warm Springs with us. It was the early 1960s and, as I've said, a uniform made her look more professional and less like just another Negro.

After high school my parents and I realized my academic background was not as strong or thorough as that of my classmates who had gone to regular school. My teacher came only once a week for two hours. I was never able to get through a whole textbook in a school year—if information was not in the first half of the book, I never learned it. I did not take Latin or other languages. I didn't take geometry or algebra. My teacher did not teach those classes and I hadn't wanted to switch teachers. I also realized I did not know much about geography, civics, or Kentucky history.

So great was our concern that I was not prepared for college that we decided I should go back to high school and take some math classes. When Mom went to sign me up, she discovered that since I had graduated, we would have to pay for the classes. That's when my mom made one of the best decisions in my life, for my life: If we're going to pay anyway, it might as well be for college.

Unbeknownst to any of us, Mom went to Kentucky Southern College, way out Shelbyville Road on the other side of Louisville. When she came home she was all excited—not because she had registered me for college, but because she had not been familiar with the highway medians of four-lane Shelbyville Road and hadn't known to pull into a turning lane. She was freaked out because a policeman had stopped her and given her a warning.

Once she calmed down, she told me that since the high school wanted money for additional classes, she had decided to go ahead and sign me up for college. I was registered for Freshman English 101 and Spanish 101, which met on Mondays, Wednesdays, and Fridays.

I almost did not get into the English class because, when she went to sign me up, it was already full. "Well, she brings her own desk and chair," my mother told them. "She has a lapboard on her wheelchair. Are you sure there isn't room for her?" They acquiesced.

I had personal attendants who enabled me to go to college: Mom and Chris to get me there; classmates to push me to class. Kentucky Southern had barely completed construction of its first building. Because it was new, the building was rather accessible: It had a loading-ramp entrance, I was given a key to an elevator, and it had one huge, accessible, unisex restroom (progressive for its day). Chris took me to my first class, Spanish 101, but I had to take care of myself the rest of the day. I had to get around on my own—with help.

Did I tell you that for years it was hard for me to ask for help? Even though Warm Springs taught me to ask for assistance if I couldn't do something and taught me to instruct people how best to assist me, they never taught me how not to feel like I was putting people out or being a burden. I didn't want to bother anyone. I began to get over that in my forties, but in college I was timid and shy. I hated asking a perfect stranger to do something for me. I would screw up my courage and ask, "Excuse me, if you don't mind, when you get a chance, if it's not out of your way, could you please . . ."

After Spanish, I had an hour an a half break before English 101. I planned to have someone push me down the hall close to the English classroom, where I would wait, out of the way, until class time. If anyone asked me why was I sitting in the hall so long, I planned simply to say: "I'm waiting for my next class. This gives me time to study."

The first day of class, after Spanish, I asked a young woman sitting close to me if she would push me to my next class. She hesitated, so I tried to be helpful by saying: "I can carry your books. Here on my lapboard." So she pushed me down the hall.

On Wednesday, I got to my second day of Spanish class early. Most people came in after I did. When the girl who had sat beside me on Monday came in, she walked to the opposite side of the room. When class was over, she left quickly with a gang of people and did not look my way, making sure I could not get her attention to ask her to push me to my next class again.

For about a week, I grabbed anyone I could to push me down the hall. Then one day, Melba, a classmate, asked if I would like to join her and her friends, Inez and Nella. They were going to the cafeteria to get lunch before their next classes. I said: "Well, yes, since you're going anyway. If you wouldn't mind pushing me." And I joined them every day that semester.

So my first real friends in college were these three middle-aged women from my Spanish class. Mothers. Friends who had encouraged each other to come back to college after raising their kids (except for Melba, who was expecting her last child). They were not concerned with cliques or clothes or most of the things college students worry about. I think they noticed a young student sitting in her wheelchair at the end of the hall by herself waiting an hour and a half for class to begin. I think they took pity on me and got me out of my corner and into the college scene.

Everyone loved and respected these women, so I looked good sitting with them in the cafeteria, the hot spot for campus socializing. My relationship with Melba, Inez, and Nella greatly affected my life. They were a bridge from adults as parents to the real world of adulthood.

For many people, high school is a defining moment; for me it was college.

Unlike my parents, who went to the University of Louisville—old, traditional, with ivy-covered buildings, huge and inaccessible—I went to a brand-new college that opened a year before I enrolled and closed a year after I left. Kentucky Southern began as a dream in the minds of a few farsighted educators. It was a co-educational college trying to be on the cutting edge of high academic standards with a blend of traditional Christian values. (Most of the farsighted educators were Baptists.) Its campus eventually held an administrative/classroom building, a student union, and two clusters of dorms.

But Kentucky Southern could compete with the colleges and universities in our state. We started out with a high ratio of Ph.D.s on our faculty, and the teacher-student ratio was good. It was southern grown, forward thinking, and passionately but politely radical. It graduated about five hundred students before it ran out of money. (Our Save Our School campaign to raise funds was unsuccessful; perhaps it was a foreshadowing of my career with nonprofit organizations and continual fund-raising.)

It was a miracle that I got to go to Kentucky Southern College, a school accessible in body, mind, and spirit. It was a perfect place for me. I met friends for life, and I began to become me.

That is what you're supposed to do in college, right? My senior
year I was president of Kenslit, the literary society; I was vice-
president of the Art Club; I helped organized the first dance on
campus for Valentine's Day, the Peace and Love Dance. My new
vocational rehabilitation counselor cautioned me: "I know extracurricular activities at college can be beneficial. But if your cur-
rent grades are a result, you'd better not be a big wheel on campus
for too long!"

I could have never been a big wheel at the University of Louisville. I would have been lost in the masses. Instead I went to a
college where I had the chance to be all that I could be.

Students who majored or minored in psych at Kentucky Southern were encouraged to see a counselor to get the feel of what
counseling was like, to better understand the concept. I developed a good relationship with the counselor, Dr. Paul Campbell,
the first person I could have an objective conversation with about
my mother.

During one of these sessions he said the most profound thing to
me. I had been ranting and raving about a recent incident: Mom
and Daddy had gone to the theater. Mom had been drinking before
they left home. When they got to the theater, Mom slipped and
fell on the lobby's marble floor and bumped her head. She didn't
really hurt herself, but she tore her stocking and she was shaken
up, so they came home early.

"Why?" I pondered out loud. "Why, during one of the few
times that Daddy wanted to be with Mom, why did she drink
and blow it?"

Dr. Campbell calmly said, "Did you ever think that maybe
your mother was afraid she couldn't compete with your father's
other women friends?" (Dad had a well-deserved reputation as a
ladies' man.) "Maybe she was afraid that if she went with him
sober and he didn't enjoy being with her, if he rejected her, she
wouldn't have the alcohol to blame." It had never occurred to me
that Mother drank because she was afraid.

I had always seen my mother as an extremely capable person. I knew she had been intimidated by law school; very few women went into law in her day. I knew she had stood up to her dad, who wanted her to be a lawyer, and became a teacher instead. She taught in a rural elementary school where some of her first graders were larger than she was, so I know she had some courage. When I was a little girl, I thought my mom seemed shy. Later I came to realize that she was being a lady, well mannered, demure. She was a 1950s housewife, making a transition into the 1960s, and it was not an easy transition for her. My mom ran our household, took care of the checkbook, and brought up us kids.

But she drank. And when she drank she was not available to me, to any of us. Dr. Campbell's comment pointed out to me, although I had never mentioned the topic to him, that it perhaps was not my fault my mother drank. Perhaps she drank because she was unhappy—not because she had a disabled kid.

Going to a counselor helped me put a lot of things in perspective. The experience also helped me—encouraged me—to move away from home. When a college friend said she admired me for going to college "in spite of my handicap," I did not know how to respond. I went to college not because I was a high achiever, not to prove I could "overcome." I went to college because my mom and dad, my uncles and aunts, all went to college. My sister did and my brother would. It was expected. It took no courage.

Moving into the dorms—that took courage. I do not know what made me decide to do it. It seems so daring to me now, although I knew a severely disabled, wheelchair-using person could live on her own. Because of my Warm Springs connection, I was getting several disability magazines. In one of them I read about a college program in Illinois set up so students with disabilities could live on campus. I was surprised at Dr. Haak's response when I mentioned it to him during my annual Warm Springs check-up. "You don't want to go there," he said. "You will live in separate housing, travel on special buses. It's a segregated program."

I guessed I didn't want that. I wanted to be like everyone else. And moving into the dorms was just the next thing to do. By my second year in college, I had begun thinking seriously about the move. I was still a freshman because I took only six hours each semester and I did not go to classes in the summer. After being in school a year, I was more comfortable with college, less timid. In my second year, I joined the freshman orientation class, participated in activities, and got to know more people.

Toward the end of that semester, my classmate Glenda commented that she was not sure she could afford to come back after Christmas. She had a scholarship but was afraid that her grades were bad and she might lose it.

Because we hung out together and had friends in common, I proposed to her that she be my attendant. I could move into the dorms, and I would pay her so she could afford to come back in January. She agreed, so I began to work on it. I talked it over with Mom; I checked it out with the college administration and Mr. Sims, the head of resident housing. Mom brought it up to Daddy, but I had to do the persuading. Yes, it was going to take a lot of planning. Yes, I was aware that it might not work out. Daddy finally agreed to pay for a dorm room and someone to help me.

I talked to Glenda before she went home for Christmas. We were supposed to talk again right after Christmas, but she did not call. And she didn't call after New Year's. So I called Mr. Sims, who told me Glenda was not coming back; her grades weren't good enough. Even though I had offered to help with expenses, she was too upset to come back to school. He had urged her to call and let me know, he said, and added that he was sorry he hadn't called me himself.

Part of me was in shock, but part of me thought, Well, it was just too much to hope for. I shouldn't be surprised; there was too much to get together to make this thing work. I felt lucky that I was getting along in college. I was more involved than in high school. I was lucky I had what I had. But it was hard telling Mom and Daddy. Mom said: "It was not very responsible of her not to

call you. I knew there was something I didn't like about her."
(Mom seldom liked anyone). It didn't really matter to Daddy; he
was probably glad to be off the financial hook.

The semester was about to begin when another friend, Darlene, offered to be my attendant. I knew Darlene better than I
had known Glenda, but she was dealing with her own disability,
manic depression. I was not sure she could do the job or should
have the job. In those days, all we knew about manic depression
was that people who had it could be moody: happy and energetic
one day, deeply depressed the next. I knew that when life got too
hard for Darlene, when she felt she couldn't take care of herself,
she checked into Our Lady of Peace Hospital and let them take
care of her.

I told Darlene she could have the job if she got someone to
share it with her. She asked me to meet with her and three potential candidates. We gathered in the dorm room that I was to
occupy—if the interviewing turned out well. The dorm room
had two of everything: beds, dressers, desks, and chairs. Before I
moved in, the room would have to be rearranged, the beds moved
out and a hospital bed that raised and lowered moved in. I decided
I would keep both dressers, but we would get rid of one desk. Each
dorm room had its own sink; I would share a bathroom with the
girls next door. The bathroom was not accessible, but I did not
really use bathrooms, so that was okay.

Darlene introduced me to the other girls. Saundra was a friend
of hers. Like Darlene, she was intelligent and artistic. She was
well traveled because her dad was in the army. Moving so much,
I'm sure, contributed to her unconventional and bohemian lifestyle. Part of the counterculture clique at my college, Darlene and
Saundra both wore black a lot; they were into poetry and art in
general. They both understood the finer things in life (although
they hadn't had many of them).

Since I was not cool or smart, I was never sure why Darlene
liked me. But she did, and I had reciprocated by taking her with
my family to our cottage at Lake Cumberland on weekends.

When she offered to take the job, she knew what she was getting into. These other girls probably had no clue. I knew Saundra well enough to be surprised that she would be interested in such a job.

I didn't know Goldie and Marsha at all. Goldie was a redhead, although over the years she tried out different shades of red. Both girls were from rural Kentucky. Marsha was slight of build and had dark, curly hair. She seemed quiet. Since Goldie was so vivacious and outgoing though, it was hard to tell if Marsha was shy or just had a hard time getting a word in.

As we chatted, it was hard to stay calm. It was dawning on me what an adventure I was about to embark upon—scary, but the next normal thing to do in the lives of people I knew. You graduate high school, you go to college, you live in a dorm. That was my goal: to live a regular life.

So here we were sitting around a dorm room talking, the girls sitting and lying on the beds. Finally, we talked about what I needed. "Well, I need everything everybody else needs. I can feed myself and brush my teeth. I need someone to get me up in the morning, pottied, washed up, dressed, and in my wheelchair, and to fix my hair."

Since I was going to hire two people, I figured that one would get me up in the morning and the other would put me to bed at night. I told the girls I would get other people to take me back and forth to classes; I would be on my own as much as I could during the day. I also told them that on Tuesdays and Thursdays, Chris would come to take care of me, do my laundry, clean my room, and help with major bathing and washing my hair. I had a lecture class on those days and I planned to send my tape recorder to class in my place. Often I did not get in my chair on Tuesdays and Thursdays.

Goldie asked if Chris could do her laundry, and I said no. She also asked if I had monthly periods. I said yes.

When I was eleven, my cousin and I had been sharing inaccurate information about menstruation. "Boy, it's really gonna be hard to keep you clean when you have your periods," she said. I was not sure what she was talking about, but at eleven I was getting used to being different. Now my cousin's comments haunted me. Evidently, Goldie was like my cousin. "Sorry," she said, "I really wouldn't be able to do the work." And she got up and left the room. Marsha went with her.

After they left Darlene admitted to me that she did not think Goldie had ever been interested in the job. "I guess she just came to hear what it was all about." I've never been comfortable talking about my personal needs; it makes me self-conscious. And now to realize I'd done all this explaining for an audience . . .

"I can do it," said Saundra. "As long as it's not mornings. I'm real hard to wake up in the morning."

So I had two girls working for me: Darlene lived in my dorm; Saundra lived in the dorm next door. Darlene got me up the morning, ready for my first class; Saundra assisted me in the evening. I do not remember how much we paid them. It wasn't a lot, but it was spending money.

When I was in my dorm room, I usually had the door open so I could get someone's attention if I needed anything. I always had my phone nearby. Many weekends I went home or to Lake Cumberland with my parents so my friends had a break.

So that Darlene could go to breakfast before coming to get me up, I never scheduled early classes when I lived in the dorms. One morning she had breakfast with a professor, got to talking, and forgot the time. Suddenly she looked at her watch and hurriedly explained to the professor that she had to leave to get me up and ready for the day. He was surprised. "I knew Cass couldn't walk," he told her, "but I didn't know she couldn't do *anything*!"

Darlene and I talked about his comment for quite a while. I certainly was not an activist, but I felt his words spoke volumes about disability consciousness. Could it be that those who knew me as a capable college student forgot about my disability? Because I seemed capable, they simply assumed I lived as they did? Is this what Mom meant when she said, "You're not like other disabled people"?

My concerns about Darlene did not prove groundless. Three weeks before the end of the semester, she had a "breakdown" and had to leave school. Saundra offered to take care of me by herself; it was difficult, but we managed. The last day in the dorms, she pushed me to my desk so I could study for my last final exam and then hurried out to her last class. My desk was cluttered with books and binders, so it was awhile before I noticed the little gray envelope propped against the wall behind the lamp. A small crystallized stone sat in front of the envelope.

> Dear Cass,
>   This, dear admirer of unusual rocks, is a little chunk of salt rock I bought at the salt mines of Berchtesgaden, Germany. Touch it to your tongue. These past few months as your "lady-in-waiting" have been an enjoyable and learning experience for me. Thank you.
>   Saundra

She thanked me! Taking care of me was enjoyable! A rewarding experience! I was moved and humbled. I felt, perhaps for the first time, that taking care of me was not a burden. I knew it was not a burden to Chris, because she got paid for it and she had grown to love me. Saundra got paid for it, too, but she was telling me it benefited her beyond pay. I was beginning to feel a little like Franklin Roosevelt: People were honored to be with me, too.

Like almost everyone else, after college I tried to get a job. It was the late Sixties. There was no disability awareness or laws. No one in my community would hire a teacher in a wheelchair. But I had lots of friends, and my life was interesting and active.

Most of my friends from college lived in Louisville, and all had jobs or were going to graduate school. I became notorious for trying to get them to take a day off, to take long weekends. My parents went to their cottage at the lake almost every weekend, spring, summer, and fall, and at least once a month in the winter. If I did not want to go, I had to find ways to stay home. My brother, M.C., was still in high school and had a busy social life so he didn't go to Cumberland much. As long as he was around, I had someone to put me to bed at night. Sometimes I depended on an agency like We Sit Better for a couple of hours of assistance; I learned early on that if you could get the same person each time, it worked out a lot better.

Whenever possible, I got my college friends Janet or Saundra or Glenda to spend the weekend. We had friends over for dinner; we had parties. Saundra once put up a sign backstage at Actors Theatre of Louisville, where she worked, announcing a party at my house on Kenwood. A band came and set up on my screened porch. All the actors came. They thought I was giving them a cast party. Each thanked me personally!

When I started having friends take care of me on weekends, my parents were a bit concerned, but Mom was relieved that she could go to the cottage and not have to take care of me. My friends and I were careful on those weekends; everyone cherished this house—and the opportunity it presented us. Janet claimed, correctly, that when Mom came home Sunday evening, the house was cleaner than when she had left on Friday—although once she did find spaghetti on the kitchen ceiling. And once—when Mom and Dad came home early Sunday night—a couple of weekend visitors were still here.

While I was having a good time, I did not want to live with my parents all my life. My friends had jobs, apartments; they had begun working on their careers. They may have had problems, but they were their own problems, while most of mine were the result of my parents' not getting along. Mom drank a lot; Daddy many nights didn't come home for dinner. On those nights, Mom had no reason to stay up. Since I needed her to get me ready for bed, I had to go to bed when she did, sometimes by eight o'clock. But I did not have to go to sleep; I had a TV with a remote control, and I had a phone close by so I could talk to friends.

During that time, I began hearing about independent living. I did not associate with people with disabilities, other than my friend Janet. But I was on the Warm Springs mailing list, and I got publications like the *Rehabilitation Gazette* and *Accent on Living*. For the first time, I started to see that many disabled people had their own hired and paid attendants, not their mom or a mother figure, not nurses, not classmates.

These people were not rich. They sometimes used unconventional means to accomplish it, but they were independent. One person I read about moved in with a couple who could not keep up their house payments; he paid them as attendants and saved their home. One woman used a respirator and motorized wheelchair; she was a hospital administrator and lived in a dorm at the hospital. She never had to worry about attendants!

I envied those people because they had control over their lives—independence. I was not sure I could ever have that at home with my mom and dad. Something had to change. My mom really couldn't take care of me, and I could not spend all my weekends away from home visiting friends.

I thought of killing myself, but I did not want to die; I just wanted a change. Glenda, who had graduated college and was a social worker at a family agency, recommended that I see a counselor at her agency, Mrs. Elizabeth Scott.

Since Daddy did not believe in counseling as a solution to any problem, I was determined to pay the bill myself. I worried about the cost. Counseling in college was free, but I was not in college anymore. When I called Mrs. Scott to make an appointment, I explained that my parents usually paid my expenses but I was doing this on my own. Luckily, since my income consisted of only thirty dollars a month from my parents, I qualified for free counseling.

Mrs. Scott reminded me of Dear Abby—or my mom, if my mom had pursued a career. She was poised and proper, caring and sincere. Her dark hair was styled. I am sure she went to the beauty parlor once a week, like my mom. At our first meeting, she told me she had helped other people find attendants; we just had to be careful and check people out. She felt bad, she said, about a client who had hired someone who turned out to do drugs and "even sold drugs!" She was talking about pot. It was the seventies; you could hardly go anywhere social without noticing drugs. I needed more than two hands to count the people I knew who did recreational drugs. I did not tell this to Mrs. Scott.

Over the next several weeks, Mrs. Scott and I talked about what it would take to move out on my own. She could help me find a live-in attendant, she said, but I had to find an apartment, money to pay expenses, and the courage to talk to Daddy about all of it.

That's where my big sister came in. Two and a half years older than I, Ann is intelligent and pretty. She was the first grandchild for both sets of our grandparents, so she was spoiled—until the rest of us came along. While I was in the hospital or the back bedroom or Warm Springs, Ann was in the middle of whatever parents go through when a child becomes seriously ill or disabled. Shortly after I had polio, Ann went away to boarding school. Mother seemed excited about it. "You are so lucky," she told Ann. "I've always wanted to go to a private boarding school." I think it was a way to get Ann out of the house so Mom would have less responsibility, and I am sure Ann looked at it as punishment. Meanwhile, I enjoyed packing "CARE" packages of cookies, gum, toothpaste, and such to mail her.

I do not remember us being close as children. Before I became disabled, I was too young to join Ann's crowd, and afterward, I couldn't even try to tag along. We became close after she married and started a family.

Ann was the best big sister I could have had, a role model for me and my college friends. We wanted a house like hers, a family like hers; she was a homemaker in the best sense of the word. She gave the best parties with great food and charm. Even my friends who may have thought she was too conventional still wanted to go to her parties—or wanted to marry her. My sister was liberal and socially conscious. She marched with other mothers to get sidewalks for a local high school and was one of the testers when Louisville worked to desegregate housing.

She never acted like a mom with me, but she did do some mom kinds of things. She could talk to Daddy.

Ann was the one who set up the family meeting when we all talked about my "problem" and my desire to move out on my own. Ann, my brother, M.C., Daddy, and I met at Ann's for dinner. We did not ask Mom because, even though my moving out would affect her life greatly, she was going through a drinking period and could not help in this.

It was an emotional time: I was still not good at asking for what I needed. This was like moving into the dorm, only bigger; there were more elements to put in play. This would be life changing for all of us. When Daddy finally said, "Okay, how much is this going to cost me?" we knew he was resigned to my move.

Now I needed to get serious about finding someone to live with me. That person, I decided, should be someone new, not a relative or friend, but someone who would sign on for the job and a place to live. I decided that any candidate would have to live with me at my parents' house for a month on a trial basis to see if we liked each other, if she could do the work, and then we could decide. Mrs. Scott was impressed with my plans for moving out. I told her disability teaches planning for contingencies.

Mrs. Scott helped me find a woman who was a resident at Central State Mental Hospital. Willie was a fifty-three-year-old divorcee with two teenage sons who lived with their father. She was at Central State because she had been "suffering from menopausal problems," I was told. She would soon be released, though, needed a place to live, and had done this kind of work before.

I did not know that such institutions cannot tell you the real reason for a resident's institutionalization. That is privileged information. But I believe that even had I known Willie was a paranoid schizophrenic, I would have still hired her.

Willie and I talked on the phone. Then she came to my parents' house for an interview. We met in my bedroom. I did not have a motorized wheelchair in those days, so I did not get in my wheelchair except to wash my hair or go out. (That's why I'm not surprised that FDR directed the country from his bed.)

Willie told me, "I'm here to do the things that you'd do for yourself if you could but you can't." I almost hired her immediately, on the strength of that comment alone, but I was trying to be professional. We talked about what I needed, about my plan to move into my own apartment. I told her that Chris would come two days a week to give Willie days off and that we could arrange other times off as needed. I told her I would still go to Cumberland and visit friends as much as I could. She said she did not need much time off; she was used to working for people in their homes. She didn't like store clerk jobs, she told me, because there were too many people to deal with and too much pressure.

After a month with Willie living at my parents' home, I hired her as my attendant, to live with me in an apartment. Moving into the dorm was easy compared to this. This was *really* scary. I was leaving my parents' home to move into a wonderful apartment in the neatest part of town—with an almost total stranger.

The first night, in bed in the biggest room in the apartment, in the dark except for the streetlights shining through my big living-room windows and into my bedroom, listening to the strange noises of this new neighborhood, I thought: What am I *doing* here?

But as scary as this might be, it wasn't as frightening as thinking of my mother and me growing old together.

This was a new world to me. And when Willie had told me, "I'm here to do the things that you'd do for yourself," she meant it. One night she fixed dinner for me and Jerry and then excused herself and went to her room for the evening—a real "lady-in-waiting." I felt elitist again, and yet I was just living my own life—at last.

I was almost thirty years old. Willie was the first person I'd actually hired as a personal care attendant (although Mom wrote the paycheck). And I finally had my own place. I could put my own pictures on the walls. I could hang plants in the windows and have big pots of plants on the floor. When I told Chris my plans, she said, in her best motherly voice, "You should be careful, now, getting all those plants and things. That'll make it harder for someone to take care of you.

"Be grateful for what you have now," she went on. "Don't make too much work for other people."

I love Chris. But when I heard her words, I felt like something was being snatched away from me. If I needed help from other people to do it, she implied, I could not have it. Underneath my reaction was the knowledge, left over from my childhood, that I was not supposed to be a burden.

Maybe that's why I saw my relationship with Willie as something like a marriage. We pooled our resources; we provided for each other. I gave her a home, income, security; I took care of her, too. She gave me independence. And my own life.

We were together one and a half years and then she decided to find someone closer to her age to work for. I think she wanted companionship.

Next I hired a college student, another resident at Central State. Lynda was closer to my age; like Darlene, she could not handle life's pressures. We had an interview and several good phone conversations, but the day she was supposed to move in, she didn't show up. I called her counselor, and he became very angry. He called her up, fussed at her, and made her call me to apologize. She told me that her counselor was right, that she was afraid of the responsibility but she did want the job. I told her she needed to make her own decision, not to come because he browbeat her. I told her if she was not happy with our arrangement, she wouldn't be able to do a good job.

She took the job.

Lynda was not the homebody Willie had been. Her life was active, with college and friends. We had to work around her class schedule, and she wasn't great at coming home on time. But the job was not hard. After a year, I tried to convince her to go to graduate school—which could have given us two more years together—but she decided she wanted her own apartment. And how could I, of all people, not understand that?

Michael, who later drove me and his sisters to visit Warm Springs, was my third attendant. If you don't count my brother and father and the next-door neighbor, he was my first male attendant. We met the night his best friend, Harold, came to Louisville to meet me and some of my friends at an Iron Butterfly concert. I was interested in Harold, so I had told him that since I would sit in the aisle and not use my ticketed concert seat, he should move down from the bleachers once the concert started and sit with us in my unused seat.

When he arrived, though, he said he couldn't join us because he had come with his best friend, and he did not want Michael to sit alone. Since Janet had come to the concert with her own chair too, we actually had two vacant seats. So Michael joined us, bringing with him two white roses. He gave one to me and one to Janet. We were impressed—until we found out the roses were for two girls he had expected to run into at the concert.

After the concert we all went to Darlene's apartment to party. Darlene's boyfriend was big, and often we would leave my wheelchair in the car and he would carry me into her apartment and sit me on the couch in the living room. That night, besides giving me a rose he had brought for another girl, Michael sat beside me on the couch most of the evening asking questions about Janet. Still, I was extremely attracted to him.

Michael and I wrote letters to each other, infrequent but long, full of philosophy and dreams for the future. I worked on each of mine for days. When it was perfect and legible, I'd send it off to him, and often the very next day I would get a letter from him. We were writing to each other, thinking about each other, at the same time. Our relationship grew.

We had traveled together, so Michael was used to my needing personal assistance. When he lost his factory job and I had not found anyone to replace Lynda, he suggested moving in with me and becoming my attendant. We had been friends for almost ten years.

When I mentioned the idea to my dad he said, "You don't have to marry him, do you?" No, Daddy! When I told Maw-Maw, my grandmother, she thought about it for a moment and said: "Well, it's probably good to have a man in the house. You'll feel safer."

Michael was tall and dark, Eric Clapton and George Harrison all wrapped up in one. He was my brother's age, really nice—and he played the drums!

We were never everything to each other, but we have been and always will be many things to each other. Together, we each became something we could have never been on our own.

Michael was the first person who let me be the most I could be. He made it possible for me to become who I was going to be. He took most of the physical barriers away, and I became a very active person as a result. Without him I could have never gotten involved with disability organizations, gone to public meetings, or been able to travel.

One day, after a meeting with Mary Johnson, when I was just beginning to be enticed by the idea of community organizing and disability advocacy, I told Michael if I got more involved with Mary's organization, I was going to have to go to more meetings. We did not have a car; when we went to meetings, Michael put my wheelchair in the back seat of a cab and his bike in the trunk. Since he wasn't interested in the meetings, he took off on his bike and visited friends in the neighborhood.

Working with this organization could mean traveling out of town, I warned Michael. If I was to get involved, I would need him a lot. If he couldn't do it or didn't want to do it, I told him, please tell me no.

I wanted him to say yes, but, in all honesty, it really did not matter to me. I was so happy to be in my own apartment, with Michael and good friends and an active social life. Anything more would have meant that I was truly lucky. "I can't do it without you. I don't have to do it—but I can't do this, I can't make this kind of commitment, unless you help me," I told him. Michael said he would.

Many times Michael made sacrifices for me. And many times I made sacrifices for him. One of those was moving to the country. Michael had grown up in Racine, Wisconsin, and in rural Kentucky. He felt that our lives would be less stressful and he would be more comfortable if we lived in the country. So in the late 1970s we moved. Moving to the country was a phenomenal undertaking. To convince Daddy that it was a reasonable idea, I argued that he was just paying rent to a different landlord. We had a used van (Daddy paid for it), I was making some money from part-time advocacy work, and I had a monthly Social Security check. I was right when I promised him it would not cost any more financially. But it did cost more.

We moved to a rental house on a horse farm in Prospect, Kentucky. The property had four houses; we took the one at the end, farthest from the main road. Our house had originally been a three-room country cottage but by then it was five rooms, plus a second bathroom for the master bedroom. The living room and master bedroom were huge. I took the bedroom, and Michael took the living room. For the first time I had a bathroom of my own.

The problem with living in old farmhouses is that often the landlords do not want to put money into them. We had problems heating the old, uninsulated house and paying for oil and propane. One winter, Michael and I put a mattress on the floor of the dining room and closed off the other rooms so we could save fuel.

Living in the country was difficult because we were so far from town. By then I had a motorized wheelchair, and I continued to be involved with disability activities. I just planned better; when I was in town, I tried to schedule several meetings and stayed downtown the whole day. But we were too far out for city buses, and Chris could not get to us to give Michael time off. Michael's having to get up early and go to the Prospect Shopping Center to pick up Chris from the Greyhound bus stop defeated the whole purpose of his having time off.

The only other way to give Michael a break was for me to go visit friends or to a party and spend the night. Sometimes I spent the night at Michael's mom's on a recliner in her living room. Michael's two brothers and three sisters, all in their teens, had lots of friends—so having someone sleep in the living room was not unusual.

I also started staying by myself a lot. I got set up for the evening with food and the phone nearby, the dining-room table stacked with files, reports, magazines, and my Talking-Book Library tape player. I learned to stay in my wheelchair all night. Michael left a couple of small pillows on a chair nearby where I could reach them if I wanted to lean over the table and put my head down, if I wanted to sleep.

Staying up in my wheelchair made me feel extremely independent. I could work all night if I chose. I could work in peace and listen to whatever music I wanted, as loud as I wanted. And in the morning, since Michael would prop the doors open before he left, I could go out on the porch and into the yard; I could hear the birds come awake, see the sun come up, and watch the haze rise off the fields.

There is joy in sitting alone in the country. It is poignant and emotional: watching the world before me change. I felt joy out on the porch, straining my eyes to see the beginning of day. Is it my imagination or is becoming brighter over there? It was a joy to watch the world change colors as the sun rose. It was astonishing to hear the nighttime sounds change to morning sounds.

I was surprised one day when Jewell called me. At that time, we hadn't worked together. We were barely acquaintances. We chatted awhile until I finally asked, "How come you're calling me?"

"Because I think you need a friend," she told me. And she was right. She knew I was isolated. Being alone in the country brought pain as well as joy. Even in a big family in the city, Jewell too was isolated. Like me, she needed independence and proper attendant services.

Although I loved being with and living with Michael, being dependent on someone who is not paid properly for the job, who is not given much time off or other benefits, is a bad situation. Friends used to say that when you pay people to work for you, they should do what you need. I never could explain adequately that when you are not paying people good wages, you try to make it up to them in other ways. Often you end up making sacrifices— like not getting a shower as often as you should, not going to the potty all day, or staying up all night in your chair.

Tonight in Claudette's backroom, Michael's "we've been through worse" echoed in my ears. Claudette's thirteen steps and tiny back bedroom were nothing compared to being in Prospect with a snowstorm raging outside (ten inches already on the ground), refrigerator and cabinets nearly bare, contemplating calling the Red Cross to helicopter me out. And since Claudette thought personal assistance was a normal thing, being here felt normal.

And being back in my mom and dad's house on Kenwood Hill felt normal. In 1984, when I moved back in, I was quick to point out to people that my parents did not live there anymore. As a child in a wheelchair in Kenwood, I hardly ever went out. But now I had a motorized wheelchair. I could get around the house and the yard. Many of the neighborhood sidewalks had curb ramps. Where they didn't, I used driveways or rolled down the less traveled side streets.

I often went to the grocery five blocks away and bought food with the help of store clerks. With my purple bag and my leather pouch, a grocery bag in my lap, I could get almost all the groceries we needed. Most Fridays I went to the bank a mile from my house. I would stop at Hardee's for a chicken sandwich and eat it there. I would stop by the shopping center and go to the drugstore, maybe browse the clothing shop, and definitely stop at the bakery. On my own. In my motorized wheelchair. Because

Kenwood was so much more accessible than any other place I had lived, my immediate world became wide open to me.

And Michael and I enjoyed the house. (It was warm!) We had parties again; we worked in the yard. I became involved with disability advocacy and volunteering at the Center. It felt like a real job—not a nine-to-five job, but for several days a week, I was busy. For years I had fought for wheelchair-accessible public buses; on Kenwood Hill, only three blocks from a bus stop, I could enjoy the fruits of that labor.

Because I was near a bus stop, attendants became more accessible. Chris came back to work for me two days a week. I did not need her for personal care but to clean, iron, and handle other housekeeping chores. And I had Claudette.

I was living a pretty normal life. And that's all I ever wanted.

"Hey!" Claudette called from her kitchen. I jumped and gasped; she had scared me. "Hey! Are you going to read all night? If we're going walking tomorrow, we better pack your stuff up tonight. Are you still reading the same book? What do you think of it?"

Should I tell her I envied Franklin Roosevelt, with his attendants? Envied how easy it seemed for him to have what he needed? All that weekend at Claudette's, I kept thinking about the difference between Roosevelt's attendants, who seemed such a natural part of his life, and the attendants ordinary people use.

Since disability folks were gearing up for another funding battle with our Kentucky legislators for our state attendant program, I was looking for an argument that gave meaning to what we were trying to do for people with disabilities.

"We never thought of the President as handicapped," Gallagher quoted a Roosevelt family friend. "We never thought of it at all." If Roosevelt had not hidden his disability, maybe people would have known how much personal assistance he needed. He acted like a nondisabled person. He did most of what he wanted. He had what he needed: Sometimes it was a valet or a Secret Service man; sometimes it was help to walk; sometimes it was help to get in bed. But he succeeded. If people understood this, they would understand that needing assistance does not mean a person is helpless.

That's a good argument, but how to overcome the fact that Roosevelt hid his disability? No one realized he could not get in bed by himself. Some people realized he faux walked, but few knew (and the public didn't know at all) that he couldn't be left alone, in case he needed something. Roosevelt walked so he would seem capable to a society that thought walking was important. The problem, as he perceived it, was being seen as a cripple, that is, unable to walk. In society's eyes, he knew that branded him as incapable. I believe it is hard for people, even today, to hold in their minds the contradictory thought that a person can be powerful and valuable to society, and at the same time, be "helpless" and dependent on others. I think Roosevelt said to himself: "If that's what it will take to convince you I'm capable, then I'll do it." He "walked," and he called himself a "cured cripple." People believed him. He "walked," and he got the jobs he wanted: governor of New York and president of the United States.

Faux walking is "passing," and passing is not good. Hiding one's disability is a bad thing. (But even as a child, I knew why Roosevelt did it.) But the "passing" was part of his legend, too. Some people do not see Roosevelt as a disability hero. Some disability activists criticize him, suggesting he is a bad model. For me, Franklin Roosevelt works as a model. For all kinds of issues: think about FDR and access, FDR and personal assistance services! Think of FDR at work and all the "reasonable accommodation" he needed. Franklin Roosevelt ran the country from his bed. To me, that is a disability hero.

Roosevelt had about him a gimp mystique; to people with disabilities, it is what Friedan's "feminine mystique" is to women. Just as the feminine mystique confined women by putting them on pedestals, by treating them like delicate creatures that needed protection, the gimp mystique limits people with disabilities.

The gimp mystique has disabled people, men and women, on pedestals, but we have to prove that we are worthy, that we belong up there. We have to get up on the pedestals ourselves, and we have to behave while on those pedestals. Roosevelt had the resources to do that.

The gimp mystique is an attitude that society has toward people with disabilities that oppresses our country's largest minority: It says we are not okay as we are. If we cannot prove we can live life on our own, we are not valid. If we have no value, providing personal assistance to us seems like a luxury—not a necessity. And we believe it. That's what makes it so hard for people to take pride in disability. The gimp mystique has to do with self-image and denying a part of ourselves. But the result of the whole "passing" effort is that it tires us out and it diminishes us.

Sometimes I think people with disabilities do not believe we have a right to a normal life. Sometimes I think the shame of needing personal assistance is so deep, millions of us do not get out of bed. "Not being a burden" is kind of hard to accomplish if you are severely disabled like Roosevelt was and I am. It seems to me that most of us who need personal assistance internalize the belief that we are being a burden to others because we need such assistance. I do not think Roosevelt saw himself as a burden to others.

The "attendant service" issue is sometimes more about self-worth than about anything else. And maybe that is the crux of the gimp mystique. The problem will not go away until every disabled person can get to the point where she believes that even having somebody wipe her bottom does not make her lesser being.

The difference between Roosevelt and most disabled people was power and money. Our degree of success at living a "normal" life has more to do with resources than with disability. Assistance for those of us without wealth and prestige has an altogether different look to it. It looks like Claudette's back bedroom.

Monday morning, the third day of my stay at Claudette's was bright and sunny. Again, Claudette got me pottied and dressed and in my chair before Dave got up and off to work. We had the rest of the day to ourselves. My bus ride home was not until eight. I didn't want to stay out that late but, in those days, you learned to compromise to get a ride. I knew Mr. Rhodes had dialysis every Monday, Wednesday, and Friday, and his TARClift bus trip from the dialysis center to home was at eight. As long as I was near the downtown area and I did not mind riding all the way out to his house, I could usually get a ride.

Mr. Rhodes was a retired executive who lived in the east end of town in a subdivision of big expensive, modern, all-electric houses. I found it interesting that this man, by all indications rich, would ride a public bus. I had ridden with enough people coming or going to dialysis to know how often they felt worn out, shaky or dizzy after treatment. Why would Mr. Rhodes take a bouncy bus under such circumstances? He should have had a limo and a personal assistant. Did he, like my dad, grow up in the depression? Was it hard for him to spend money on himself? "Special transportation" for the handicapped or cabs cost about $25 one way. For dialysis, you are talking about $25 six times a week—or $150.

As was the rule, the TARClift bus would drop you off at the curb; you had to make your way from the street into your house. Usually the driver would wait until he saw Mrs. Rhodes open the door; then we would know Mr. Rhodes was safe inside. The driver told me he once couldn't wait—because of the schedule—and Mr. Rhodes fell and his wife had to call 911. I am sure Mr. Rhodes did not expect retirement to be like this.

That day at Claudette's, I had awakened with an ache in the pit of my stomach, the kind I feel when I have to give a workshop or presentation. I was excited about running around my old neighborhood with Claudette, but I was scared of the ramps outside the kitchen door. I sat at the top of what looked like a ski jump (although these ramps did not turn upward at the bottom). The hill on the campus at Warm Springs seemed gentle compared to this. Even if Michael were here, I would still have been afraid. This was one of those times when you "have nothing to fear but fear itself." And the fear was just about killing me. Okay, I reasoned, if you die, you die. And if there is a next time, make sure the people helping you know how to get you down overly steep ramps.

I sighed audibly when we touched the ground, ecstatic that I had made it and relieved that I did not have to use ramps anymore. Claudette, Luke in his stroller, and I headed through the backyard, down the alley, and toward Cherokee Road. Claudette's house was about ten blocks from my old apartment, our eventual destination, but we planned to make several stops along the way.

I was so excited. Cherokee Road looked the same but different. I seldom went on walks when I lived here, so I seldom saw it from this perspective. I realized how different life would have been if I had owned a motorized wheelchair when I lived here.

I did not get a motorized wheelchair until I was thirty-two years old, when Vocational Rehab paid for it. We talked seriously about getting me one during high school but Mom said they didn't work well on tile, they slowed down on rugs; they were heavy; and we would have to get a van. My parents did not think it was a good use of our money. If we had been rich, I think they would have bought me one.

Here I was, in my old neighborhood, strolling down the sidewalk in my motorized wheelchair, with Claudette and Luke in his stroller following behind. I wondered what onlookers thought of us. A mom, daughter, and grandson? A mom, a son, and a nanny? Sisters? Friends going to lunch?

Actually, that morning Claudette had been my employee. Now it was afternoon and we were friends taking a walk and running errands. We were going to the branch library so Claudette could take library books back, we planned to do a little antiquing (my best furniture came from an antique store on Bardstown Road), and we wanted to find someplace to eat lunch.

When we got to the library, I realized some things had not changed at all. The building was not accessible, almost ten years after federal regulations said it should be. I joked with Claudette that it was not a problem since I didn't have any books to go back. I said I would wait outdoors and work on my tan. "Just take Luke with you," I urged.

Ironic, I thought, that it should be this library. When I lived in my first apartment on Cherokee Road, my polling place was in the basement of this same inaccessible neighborhood branch. The Democratic precinct captain was so anxious for me to vote that he came to my apartment and took me to the polls himself. The walk over was rough. I did not have a motorized wheelchair and there were no curb ramps. We mostly stayed in the alleys.

When we reached this building, the precinct captain and the guys who helped him carry me and my wheelchair down the steps became instant access advocates. I hesitated to make any reference to President Roosevelt being carried, but I did point out to them—halfway back up the stairs after I voted—"You know, it really shouldn't be this hard to vote!"

4   The Radicalization of Cass

There are counselors these days who say: "Do nothing"; other counselors who say: "Do everything." Common sense dictates an avoidance of both extremes. I say to you: "Do something," and when you have done something, if it works, do it some more; and if it does not work, then do something else.
—Franklin D. Roosevelt, 1936

THE FIRST disability article I published, in the *Rehabilitation Gazette* magazine in 1977, was called "The Radicalization of Cass." It was about my realization that no matter how hard I worked in my chosen field (then it was teaching), I could never earn enough money to pay the expenses of living with a disability. Society was structured in such a way that I could excel only so far. "Overcoming" had nothing to do with my disability and everything to do with my economic status.

I remember the first night in my apartment, a strange new place, with a woman attendant I had known for only a month. I was out from under Mom and Daddy. Just like most of my friends, I was on my own. But unlike them, I was unemployed. I had my own apartment without a job because I had financial help. My father paid for it; my father paid for the attendant.

I had no idea what was going to happen in my future. In the past, the road to employment (or to unemployment) had been bumpy and full of obstacles. After I graduated high school, I met with Mr. Binder, a vocational rehabilitation counselor, to talk

The epigraph is from Geoffrey C. Ward, *Closest Companion: The Unknown Story of the Intimate Friendship between Franklin Roosevelt and Margaret Suckley* (Boston: Houghton Mifflin, 1995), 80.

about what I wanted to do. Chris took me to the VR office downtown in the state employment office building.

Things did not have to be very accessible in those days, but government buildings made an effort. There was a long, steep ramp to the back door. Since it was the entrance mostly used by staff and for deliveries, there were no signs or directions to tell us where to go once inside. Finally, Chris and I came to a huge room of stereotypical cubicles and found Mr. Binder in the midst of this maze. When Chris left me there for my meeting, we were both concerned that she would not find her way back.

When I was young, I wanted to be a nurse. My mom was a teacher before she had children. Her sisters were teachers; one sister married a teacher. My dad's brothers were preachers, and his sisters married preachers. (Preachers' wives are really teachers, aren't they?) So I come from a family of teachers on both sides. The one thing I swore I never wanted to be was a teacher. Even after I had polio, I wanted to be a nurse.

When I was fourteen, that dream was gently reconfigured. I was floating around in the pool at Warm Springs waiting for my physical therapist, Mrs. Nottke. I had not learned to swim before I got polio but here, perhaps because of the warm pool water, I had no problem floating on my own. Sometimes I would float near the ladder, hook my arm in a rung, and tighten my tummy muscles, which made my hips go down so I would be sitting upright in the water. When I grew tired, I would relax and let my hips float back up, and I would be lying in the water floating again, paddling myself around with one arm.

I could not propel myself well and sometimes I got stuck in a corner, or worse. Once I floated dangerously close to a therapist and his patient. The therapist was from India and everyone gossiped about how stern and unfriendly he was. Men in his country did not think much of women, and even though his wife was well educated and an occupational therapist herself, she always walked behind him.

And now I was about to bump right into him. "Whoa," he said.

"I'm sorry," I replied. "I can't guide myself very well!"

He chuckled and pushed me in the direction of Mrs. Nottke. It was the first time I had ever seen him smile. He was very handsome when he smiled. One of the things I really liked about Warm Springs was that I met people from many different countries; that would have never happened at home in Louisville.

Mrs. Nottke came to my rescue and pushed my floating body over to an exercise table in the water. Our conversation got around to what I was going to be when I grew up, and I talked about being a nurse. I guess because I had been in the hospital a lot, I wanted to take care of other people, to make them feel better. Mrs. Nottke said, "Well, dear, I think you'll be very good at teaching nurses their profession." She wasn't any more specific than that. She did not say: "That's not realistic. You're never going to walk again. There's no way you're going to be a nurse." But her words made me realize that I would never be able to do the kinds of things a nurse does. I would not be able to give shots, take temperatures, make beds. I could learn the craft and teach it, but I would never be able to do those things myself. It was the first time I understood that I was not going to "get better." This was as good as it was going to get. There was no cure going on here. Just truth and reality.

By the time I met with the VR counselor, my life had been saved by a high school English teacher (who helped me overcome the gaps in my education), and my writing had been encouraged by teachers and a journalism class. So I was sure teaching was my career choice, and I hoped to eventually write magazine or newspaper articles. I think those goals were kind of typical for upper-middle-class women of my time.

Mr. Binder looked at my high school transcripts and together we filled out an application for financial assistance for college. He asked me what I wanted to do upon graduation. I told him I intended to be a teacher or a writer, maybe a journalist. He wanted to know specifics: How would I write articles? I said my handwriting was pretty clear if I wrote slowly; for articles, I told him,

I would use a tape recorder and an electric typewriter. I knew that teaching was a lot of sitting and talking, and I could do that, I told him. I was not being a smart aleck; I was simply answering what I thought he was asking.

Several days after our meeting, Mr. Binder called to tell me VR was not going to give me financial assistance for college. My grades were good, he said, but he did not think my goals to be a teacher or a writer were achievable. He thought I was "too disabled to work." He would send a confirmation letter.

Thank goodness I never told Mr. Binder I wanted to be a nurse! I believe he was the first person to ever tell me directly (albeit over the phone) that I was "too handicapped." I realized I was pretty disabled: I do not walk; I do not even stand; I do not dress myself. (When Michael and I lived in Prospect, I figured a way to get my blouse off and wash up and get a fresh blouse on, but it took a long time and I was pooped afterward.) There were millions of things I could not do, but I was sure teaching was *not* one of them.

Mr. Binder did not know me, and his lack of knowledge almost kept me from college. I think that is what made me angry. I overcame that obstacle with money from my parents, but it was only luck that they could afford to send me to college.

The summer after my first year of college, I met a secretary who worked at the same VR office as Mr. Binder. She asked me about college, and I told her that VR was not paying for it because my career goals were not attainable. She said a counselor did not have the right to make that kind of decision; the money came from a government program for disabled people and because I was disabled, I was eligible. If I did not succeed in college, then they could decide not to refund me, but Mr. Binder was wrong to refuse payment for my first year of college. She suggested I go to the head of the department and file a complaint.

I was eighteen years old and shy, but I was also angry. The more I thought about it, the more I realized the government had made a commitment to people with disabilities, and we had a right to the opportunity to get an education and become productive. Now a person who did not know had told me what I could and could not do, and he would keep me from an education.

But file a complaint? Me? Remember, I am the one who gets praised for not complaining. But I knew this was wrong. Mr. Binder was wrong. And I was going to have to do something about it.

I do not confront people easily, much less go over someone's head. I was scared to death, but I screwed up my courage and called the head of the department. Using the phone gave me some protection: If I had seen an annoyed look, I would have crumpled. The problem was that often, when I am really angry, I tear up, get a quivery voice, and nearly cry.

After listening to my almost tearful complaint, Mr. Beckhart, the head of the Jefferson County Department for Vocational Rehabilitation, hemmed and hawed and finally said, "We'll look into it." The result was they asked me to go for testing to see if I was "college material." By this time, I had completed a year of college and I had a B average. You would have thought that might be proof enough. The testing, I think, was to save face for my counselor.

I was sent to Jewish Family and Vocational Counseling Services downtown. By now, Mom had given up driving me everywhere. She had decided it was silly for her to go, since Chris could drive, and then Mom could rest up all day and be energetic enough to make dinner when, or if, Daddy came home.

Getting to the office was a hassle. There was parking nearby where an attendant drove your car up into the garage. It was awkward for us, because Chris had to get me out of the car before the attendant could park it. I was not comfortable getting out of the car in front of people. I have never liked audiences.

We called the technique we used to get me out of the car "plus one." Chris turned me sideways in the front seat so my legs were outside the car; she locked my long leg braces; then she leaned over, grabbed the back of my waist or my back brace—whatever

was convenient—stood back, and pulled me up to her in a standing position. We rocked back and forth, moving one leg forward
or back as necessary, until she backed me up to the wheelchair.
Then she would lean forward, my hips would bend, and I would
be sitting in my chair.

To make matters worse, the parking attendant would stand
there, waiting, every time we went. He was cute and I am a flirt—
especially when I think there is no chance the object of my flirta-
tion will take me up on it. But instead of feeling flirtatious, I was
embarrassed to have him see such a spectacle. I wanted to shout:
"Wait, don't judge me by this! When my brother takes me places,
he just picks me up. It's usually less awkward than this!"

Getting in and out of the car observed by a cute spectator was
the worst part of these excursions to town. The rest was kind of
fun. It consisted of four days of tests, which VR paid for. Since
we were downtown anyway, Chris and I would shop a little and
sometimes get something to eat on the way home.

The counselor giving the tests, Mr. Summers, was cute as
well. He was slight of build, with dark hair, black-rimmed Buddy
Holly glasses (not old-fashioned in those days); he wore a white
short-sleeved shirt, tie, navy trousers, and penny loafers. I flirted
with him, big time. But it was safe because he also wore a big
gold wedding band and had a prominent photo of his wife and
baby on his desk—we both knew I was joking. We started out
with an interview. I told him about the events that preceded this
meeting; he told me I would take a battery of vocational aptitude tests, IQ tests, general aptitude tests. The results would be
sent to VR.

I do not mind taking tests, except muscle tests, which mean a
lot of poking and one therapist saying to the other, "Weak?" "No I
think that's a trace, not stronger than that." In those days muscles
were rated normal, good, fair, poor, or trace, and the results had
a lot to do with the sensitivity of the tester.

I worried some about multiple-choice tests, because I often got
stuck between two answers and always chose the wrong one. Be-

fore I took any written tests, I pointed out to Mr. Summers that writing was physically hard for me and if I was rushed, my handwriting became illegible. In college they gave me extra time for tests and essays. He made a note about that. There were speed tests where I put a puzzle together, or put colored blocks in the right order and pattern. I asked Mr. Summers if I got twice as much time since I could only used one hand. He said he would compensate for that in his scoring and made another note.

I feared the IQ tests, though, because I would not be able to hide my lack of education. During these tests, when Mr. Summers asked me questions like, "How does yeast make bread rise?" I explained to him that my education had been a bit sparse because it was home instruction, so I never had a science class. He asked me to try to answer anyway, so I told him that it was the natural tendency of yeast, when mixed with water, to rise. He smiled and wrote something down.

I also had to draw three pictures: one of my house, one of my family, and another of a tree. I worried about this because I am an artist: I am creative and my house is unusual. So I drew my house with the round window in the kitchen, the bay windows in the dining room, and the three sets of windows in the living room. I drew our big yard and long driveway. I drew my mom, dad, big sister Ann, little brother M.C., my brother's dog Butch, and myself in the wheelchair. I drew a huge tree (we have a huge oak tree in our yard) with big branches and squirrels—and I drew a hole in the tree full of nuts. It bothered me, sort of, to think that he was looking at all of this in some sort of psychological way. But I was proud because the pictures I drew were elaborate and artistic.

When the tests were over, Mr. Summers scheduled an appointment to give me the results. He showed me the IQ scale and asked, "Where do you think you fall on this chart?" I was self-conscious about answering. I realized from my family background, my parents' education, and my education so far that I should be among the top 10 percent. But I was afraid I would not measure up because my education had been incomplete. So, to keep myself from embarrassment, I pointed to the middle.

Mr. Summers smiled. "You are smarter than that," he said, and showed me where I fell on the scale. I was no genius but I was well above average. I was amazed. The tests also showed I should work in a helping profession. Mr. Summers thought I would be a good teacher, if that is what I chose, or a social worker—maybe a vocational counselor. The test results, he said, showed that I had the ability to attend college and I would benefit positively from the college experience. That was what he would report to VR.

Because of that report, VR paid for my college education and for books and supplies until I graduated—as long as I kept my grades up.

In college I took the classes required to get a teaching certificate and I completed student teaching. This meant spending a semester observing a teacher in the classroom, working with the teacher to develop lesson plans, and eventually taking over the classes with the teacher supervising. For this, I earned nine hours of college credit; the supervising teacher determined the grade.

Student teaching almost became an obstacle to my becoming a teacher. Neither the city nor the county public school systems would allow me to student teach at their schools. If we let you student teach, their argument went, it's as though we're going to hire you, and we won't, because we don't hire teachers in wheelchairs. That did not seem right, but there was nothing I could do about it. There was no government mandate for employment as there was for an education.

Finally, the Catholic school system agreed to let me do student teaching if I could get a principal's permission. The closest Catholic high school was only four blocks from my house—within walking distance. It was a boys' school, my brother's school, where he was a track star and president of his senior class—and he was not even Catholic. I decided this school was not a good choice.

I called the girls' high school closest to me, but it was not accessible. The first floor had offices, the gym, and the cafeteria; all classrooms were on the second and third floors. I had been toted up and down stairs during my two years at high school, and it was scary. I would not do it as part of a job.

My second choice was an all-girls school about ten miles from home. It was fairly accessible, and the principal accepted me. Sister Mary Joseph, who taught four senior English classes and one religion class, became my supervising teacher. She had been teaching for about twenty years and had been at this school since it opened.

I was not able to get to school early enough for Sister Mary Joseph's first class at 8:30. I had to have Chris's help to get up, dressed, and to school; since she had a child to take care of, it would have been a hardship for her to come to our house at six. I could get to school about ten o'clock.

I began by observing Sister Mary Joseph's senior English classes. Whenever I could get to school earlier, I sat in on her religion class.

Chris stayed later than usual while I was student teaching because I had to be at the school until 2:30. She would pick me up, take me home, help me in bed, and set up for the evening. Usually my evenings were spent getting study plans ready for the next day or grading papers.

This was the first time I had a "regular" work day: get up, go to work, put in a full day, five days a week. It was not an eight-hour day, but the job was the most strain I had ever put on my body. In college I was careful not to take more than six hours a semester. I did not take any classes while doing my student teaching. Still, I got very tired, and I got pneumonia. I was in the hospital several days and had to be out of school for six weeks. After the new year, I came back and continued my student teaching.

Shortly after I returned, Sister Mary Joseph decided I was ready it take over a class. Three, actually—I took over three of her senior English literature classes for a full nine-week grading period.

And you know something? I think I did a good job. If disabled people have attributes as a group, one, I would say, is the ability to plan, organize, and coordinate. Disability affects how you organize and shape your life, not necessarily a negative effect. I was much better organized than Sister Mary Joseph. I had to be. I was new, and Sister had so many years of experience, she really did not have to plan; it was all in her head.

There were other differences between us. One, obviously, was age: Sister was in her fifties; I was twenty-three. My students were only six years younger than I. Sister wore matronly, dark blue clothes, with sensible old-lady shoes and a short veil. I wore the kind of clothes my students would be wearing if they were not required to wear school uniforms.

And I was M.C. Irvin's big sister. Not only was my brother a jock, but also he was handsome, a gentleman at seventeen years old. I was student teaching in the school his girlfriend attended, so all the girls knew him and most were gaga for him. This boosted my reputation immensely. Because of my relationship to M.C., I think, my students wanted to help me succeed. But there were obstacles to overcome.

Once I was in charge, I arranged for two students from my classes to meet me in the hall and take me to my first class. Because Sister Mary Joseph had seniority, all her classes (now my classes) were in the same room. I thought it was kind of cool that I put students in charge of getting me to class. I reminded them it would be their fault if I did not get to class on time.

One day as two students were pushing me to class, Sister grabbed my wheelchair and pulled me away. "Wait a minute, girls. I have to talk to Ca—uh, Miss Irvin." Sister had a hard time calling me Miss Irvin. She also had a hard time not patting me on the head in front of other teachers. One day I told her, in the most polite way, that if she did it again I would bark like a dog. From then on when she got the urge to pat me on the head, she stopped, chuckled, and told whoever was near: "Oh, I better not pat Cass on the head. She said if I ever did that again . . ." While she said this, I got looks of sympathy from all around.

Sister Mary Joseph rushed me into the front office and then into the principal's office. She closed the door. She was sort of scaring me. I thought someone had died. "What's the matter?" I exclaimed.

"Your skirt!" She started trying to pull it down. "It's so short you can see right up your skirt!"

"Sister, I'm wearing orange pantyhose. If anyone sees anything, it will be orange."

But she continued to pull on my skirt. Finally, she realized it was futile. I was not concerned. This was an all-girls school. Most of the girls wore short-skirted uniforms. Sister finally pushed me out of the principal's office, and the girls quickly got me out of the front office.

"What did she do, Miss Irvin?" They were concerned because my face was so red.

"We are going to be late," I answered. "Maybe I'll tell you later." They pushed me to class, giggling behind me all the way. I never told them.

One of the cool things Sister Mary Joseph did was show movies. She loved to show Orson Welles's *Macbeth*. And she loved to startle the students dozing off during this dark, depressing film by running it in reverse right after Lady Macbeth jumps from the cliff—making Lady Macbeth do a reverse somersault and bound back up onto the cliff. It was so irreverent of Sister, so unlike her. It got everyone's attention.

When I was in charge of the class, I was supposed to show a film also. This was long before video stores, so I had to check out a film from the downtown library. Since I did not drive and could not get the film myself, I got all the details about how to check out a film and had a student pick it up. I was supposed to run the projector, too, but I could not reach high enough to thread the film. Since Sister had shown me how to do it, I showed a student how. It was tedious, but the girls were patient. They seemed to like helping me.

One day I sat in on a seventh-grade class. The teacher was a brother and brand new to teaching. The girls barraged him with silly questions and wrapped him around their fingers. They looked at me as if to say, You know what we're doing, don't you? You won't tell, will you? How challenging, I thought, to be to be able to get and hold their attention and teach them something. I was scared to death most of the time, but I really loved teaching.

The head of the Education Department at my college dropped by to observe my classes. He asked if I had any problems. I was wondering about one thing: I could not move around the classroom to look at the students' work (this was before I had a motorized wheelchair)—did he think this put me at a disadvantage?

He told me he would prefer me to sit in the middle of the room with the students around me, sort of in a horseshoe shape. Sister was too conventional, so I could not try anything like that. He suggested that I ask the girls if my not moving around had been a problem for them. One student told me she liked it much better because, unlike most teachers, I could not sneak up on her!

At the end of my teaching assignment, Sister Mary Joseph told me she wanted to talk to me about my grade. We met in her classroom, where she said she had been quite happy with the job I had done with the girls. She liked my style of teaching, she knew the girls liked me, and she had even seen some students blossom. She said I had done everything she asked of me and she could not be more pleased.

"But I'm having a difficult time deciding between two grades," she went on. "I don't know whether to give you an A or a B." I breathed a sigh of relief. This was nine hours of college credit—I had been afraid she was torn between a B and a C, and I could not afford a C. "To me," she continued, "an A is for perfection and you, after all, are handicapped. So I feel obliged to give you a B."

I had not expected an A, but I was shocked at her reasoning. And I was angry. I talked to the head of the Education Department at my college, who, ironically, was my uncle and hard of hearing—but he said the decision was hers. There was nothing he could do about it.

People talk about overcoming a disability, but the real struggle is overcoming the Sister Mary Josephs—the people who handicap us because they do not see us as capable. This stigma is debilitating. It can keep us from being who we might be. But it is not the disability itself that handicaps us.

My problems with this stigma were just beginning. Once I got a teaching certificate, I tried for a year to get a job as a teacher. I knew the city public schools would not hire me; they told me that outright when they refused my application for student teaching. I had hoped to get a job with the Catholic high school where I had done my student teaching, but it was having financial difficulties and was letting all lay teachers go.

I soon discovered that no school in the county, public or private, would hire me. Out of the dozen I applied to, only one replied—with a rejection letter. I called several school principals to inquire about my status. Only one returned my call, an assistant principal who told me snippily: "It's three weeks until school starts. I should think it's pretty obvious."

Having been so thoroughly rejected, I stopped my job pursuit and enjoyed life for a while. Mom and Daddy went to Lake Cumberland a lot. I stayed home when I could and had people over, or I visited friends.

Every so often a job prospect would come my way, often through my sister, Ann. One opportunity she found was a job as the director of a church daycare center only ten blocks from my home—easily doable in a motorized wheelchair. I was beginning to think seriously about getting one.

I spoke to the church secretary, Mrs. Rice, and set up an interview. Chris took me to the appointment. By now we had decided the long leg braces were a hassle; it was easier for Chris to lift me in and out of the car and put me in my wheelchair.

I had explained to Mrs. Rice over the phone that I used a wheel-chair and asked the best way to get into the building. She told me the daycare center was in the basement of the church; there was one ground-floor entrance, down about three steps. (She was wrong—there were six.) Because of the steps, I should have never considered the job, but when you have been looking for work for a year and a half and when all your friends are working and you have not had any offers, you accept less than ideal conditions. I thought that if I got the job, I would get Daddy to build a ramp.

Chris tipped my wheelchair back on its big back wheels, and we went down the steps to the basement. In the daycare facil-ity, Mrs. Rice gave us the grand tour. There were three rooms for classes, a kitchen and dining area, a storage room, and the direc-tor's office, where Mrs. Rice conducted my interview. She gave me an overview of the program and explained that the outgoing director left because her husband had a stroke and she wanted to stay home with him. Mrs. Rice was very talkative.

My job would be to oversee the program, compile records, pay bills. The church had a volunteer accountant, but I would do all the rest. The two teachers currently employed had both been there over a year and were totally in charge of their classes. I would need to coordinate their schedules and check on them, but mostly, Mrs. Rice said, they knew what they were doing. We hit it off well, and I think I had a great interview. She told me I was the most qualified person to apply so far, since I had a teaching certificate.

I came home excited and a bit apprehensive. I was not sure I could handle such a job. Having pneumonia had scared me. This seemed much more strenuous than student teaching. Half of me did not want the job, but the other half wanted it, because every-body else had a job.

Finally the preacher's wife called me. She had talked to Mrs. Rice and wanted to make sure I was aware of the job responsibili-ties. First, she said, the director must open up the daycare center at 6 A.M. and could not leave until the last child was picked up at the end of the day, usually at 6 P.M.—if the parents got there on time. Also, the director was responsible for developing the lesson plans for each class and program, ordering all supplies and food items, developing the menus, scheduling all parent-teacher meetings, all class and attendance records, and reporting to the church.

It seemed like a difficult job—for anyone. The hours were long and the pay mediocre. But I was timid and desperate and everything seemed insurmountable to me. I told the preacher's wife that it was more hours than Mrs. Rice had led me to believe, but that I would find the resources (Mom, Chris, Ann?) to do the job. I sounded determined, but I did not believe myself.

A week later, I chickened out and called to take myself out of the running. Mrs. Rice answered the phone. "Well, dear, I've been meaning to call you. We found someone else to do that job."

I was so relieved! I was also curious about who they had hired. I found out later from Ann that the minister's wife, who was employed full time as an elementary school teacher, was going to do the job in her spare time.

Two years had passed since my graduation from college and I still did not have a job. I went back to Vocational Rehabilitation to see if they would pay for graduate school so I could get a master's degree and become more employable. Mr. Binder had moved on to other employment, and a different counselor, Mr. Vance, listened to the story of my unsuccessful attempts at getting a job. I wanted to be a teacher, I said, and I did not think I should change careers—yet. I thought that if I had a master's degree, I could teach college. I also explained that after my bout with pneumonia while student teaching, I was concerned about my physical stamina for full-time work. I reasoned that if I taught college, I could begin teaching part-time and try to work up to full time.

By now the Rehabilitation Act of 1973 was in the works; state vocational rehabilitation departments were beginning to be criticized for not serving more severely disabled people. Since I was one of those, Mr. Vance was very willing to work with me. Still, VR decided I would have to get a physical exam to determine if I had the stamina to work.

Another day of testing. Another trip to town. I was told to wear my leg braces, since the doctor needed to know my "true condition," but as soon as we got there, Chris had to get me out of my wheelchair and onto the narrow exam table. She had to remove my long leg braces, clothes, and back brace so I could be examined.

The doctor was a well-known orthopedic surgeon. I recognized his name but I had never met him. He was ancient. He took my right hand in his and said: "Squeeze my hand. Hard."

I could not do it. Then he took my left hand in his and said, "Squeeze my hand." I could not.

"Try," he said.

"I am trying," I responded.

I could see Chris over his shoulder. She was smiling. We both felt what he was doing was silly.

"Lift your right arm." I could lift it a little bit off the table, but I could not hold it up too long. My muscles would tire and my arm would fall back down.

"Raise your right leg . . ." Nothing.

He looked at my torso and correctly diagnosed a curvature of the spine. He examined my legs and correctly diagnosed crooked joints at the knees and ankles.

"Can you stand?" he asked.

"Yes," I told him, "with braces and crutches—and if someone stands me up and stays behind me so I do not buckle and fall."

He reported each discovery to his nurse, who would then write something on a yellow legal pad. I was not sure how this determined stamina. Before he left the room, he asked me why I had come in for an exam. I explained the stamina issue and future employment and graduate school. "Okay," he said.

Evidently he sent in the kind of report I needed. Vocational Rehabilitation paid for graduate school, which was lucky for me, because even though my dad believed in higher education, he would not pay for graduate school because he did not think anyone would hire somebody in a wheelchair—and, so far, he was right.

I went to the University of Louisville for my master's degree, my mom and dad's alma mater. I was worried about the large campus and the old, inaccessible buildings, but since I was in the graduate program, all my classes were in one place.

Again, there were obstacles. My first was a meeting with the head of the English Department, Dr. Axton. Chris and I did not know until we got to Gardner Hall that his office was in the basement, although I am sure I mentioned that I used a wheelchair when I called to find out about registration and make an appointment. It is part of my standard introduction: "Hello, my name is Cass Irvin, I-R-V-I-N, Cass, C-A-S-S, and I use a wheelchair and I am looking for . . . ," or "I need . . . ," or whatever.

Chris and I were trying to be macho again, so we just bounced down the steps. The first thing Dr. Axton did was call another advisor, who, although she had a basement office, offered to meet with me on the ground level. Then we discovered that Gardner Hall had no ground-level office space. There was only a stairwell and a hallway to the elevator. So Dr. Ricky, my new advisor, sat on the steps beside me while we filled out forms and developed my class schedule.

Two classes caused problems. One was linguistics, an introduction to phonetics and the study of sound in language. The major assignment was to interview someone about their life—a friend or family member—and record the interview on tape. We were then to transcribe the interview word for word, study it, and then transcribe it phonetically and explain what we had discovered about how our subject spoke. I could handle the tape recorder and the interview part, but the transcribing would be tedious and take me twice as long as my classmates. (I knew right away who I was going to use as my subject: Jerry, my college classmate and sometime boyfriend, always the southern gentleman, from Okolona, in Jefferson County, Kentucky—a country boy who spoke proper English and pronounced orange jam "marmalaud.")

I went to the professor, Dr. David W. Maurer, a leading scholar of American language and its social history. He was old and had begun having trouble walking. I asked Dr. Maurer if there was something I could do instead of the transcriptions. (I was not having a problem with his other class assignments.) He said he totally understood; these days it took him longer to do things. He assigned a research paper and, in the end, gave me an A for the class. I thought his attitude exemplified an understanding accommodation.

Dr. Daniels, on the other hand, exemplified something different. He taught my course in scholarly research. The goal: to become skilled at research and using reference materials. Dr. Daniels required us to review 144 library reference materials in the university's library: Locate the appropriate reference book, leaf through it, find out exactly what kind of information it contained, and then find the specific source material needed. He told us he expected us to spend at least twenty hours a week in the library. (In Cassie-time that meant thirty-five hours or more.)

Once we found the reference materials, Dr. Daniels wanted us to record on one half of an 8½-by-11-inch sheet of paper the name of the reference material, where in the library the item was found, and what it could be used for. My sister's mother-in-law thought she was helping me out by providing my paper. She had legal-size paper, which she cut in thirds with a paper cutter. I used this for recording my first batch of books, and Dr. Daniels rejected my work because the paper was not the correct size. I had to copy them over.

I was beginning to feel overwhelmed. Remember, this was in the 1970s, when reference works were big, bulky books like the *Reader's Guide to Periodical Literature,* publications of the Modern Language Association, and the *Oxford English Dictionary,* not available as they are today through modem and mouse. They sat, inaccessible, on shelves in reference rooms of libraries.

There were no automatic doors at the university. The accessible entrance to the library was in the back, up the loading-dock ramp. Inside was a freight elevator. Once Chris got me in the building, I needed someone to push me to the library, get me inside, up the elevator, into the reference room, and up to a table.

And that was just the beginning. I could not get to the bookshelves without someone pushing my wheelchair to them. I could not get the books off the shelves without assistance. Most reference books were so large and heavy that I needed help getting them open. I can use my right arm some, but it is not strong. Turning the pages took time, too; some were huge. I could do it, but much more slowly than someone whose arm worked well. Everything took me more time. A lot of time.

It soon became clear that I would never be able to turn in the assignment by the deadline. I went to the professor and asked if some accommodation could be made, perhaps a decrease in the number of reference items. He was visibly displeased and made his displeasure further known by his tone of voice. He would see what he could do about getting student helpers, he said curtly. He did find a student to help for a few hours, but trying to coordinate her schedule with mine and Chris's was difficult. It was not enough help, and by semester's end, I had not completed the assignment. I took an Incomplete for the research class and hoped I could get it done over the summer. Of course, that didn't happen—it was summer!

The fall semester I had eighteenth-century English lit, and I had to team teach a section of *Gulliver's Travels*. I was not sure I understood the section, and I knew my partner did not. I was a grad student; she was a senior. I am not usually the smart one. I was terrified to be in front of class, especially with a girl that was not as smart as I was. To make matters worse, the class was taught by Dr. Daniels, who *loved Gulliver's Travels*.

After our presentation, Dr. Daniels complimented me on my part. His positive comments about my partner's part concerned information we had developed together. I worked hard in that class and got a B. But I got nothing done toward fulfilling my Incomplete.

The following semester was the same. There was no money to pay for assistance; students did not have enough time to help me do all that was required. I eventually sought out the head of the department to see if something could be done about my Incomplete. He told me he did not like to interfere with a professor's assignment, but he would think about it.

One day, Dr. Daniels spotted me waiting outside of class and said he would accept the work I had completed so far. He would remove the Incomplete and give me a C for the class. My first thought was: Dr. Maurer gave me an A, so together they would average out to a B; my grades were safe. Dr. Daniels went on to say that he did not mind doing this, but he wished I had felt I could have come to him instead of going the head of the department. I felt embarrassed at having had to ask for help at all—it looked as though I could not do the work. In my heart, I knew the problem was not my ability but the lack of assistance. That C reflected the inaccessibility of the process I had to follow. I also felt embarrassed that he was talking to me here in the hallway, in front of other students, but, of course, his basement office was inaccessible to me.

It was during grad school that I moved into an apartment and started making a home of my own. That first year I was able to live a pretty regular life. I traveled with friends. I had people over for dinner and parties. I felt a bit like a woman of leisure, since I did not have to work. I was an unemployed grad student who had an apartment because her dad paid for it. I did not feel privileged or guilty; I just wanted what all my friends had. And, for a while, I liked not working.

Then my friend Gail came over after work one day, while I was sitting in my living room cleaning out my desk drawers. She was tired. It had been a hard day at the state employment office. After she complained about her clients for a while, she casually asked what I had been doing all day.

"Mostly I cleaned out my desk drawers," I said, which for me really *was* work. (Does that sound pathetic?) Willie had to push my chair under the desk so I could reach everything, and it is hard to pick up things; it is hard to open a heavy drawer. I had gotten set up at my desk, with the phone nearby and the front door unlocked for Gail, so Willie could go shopping. By the time Gail arrived, I had been behind the desk for about four hours.

"Oh, it must be nice. I wish I could stay home and clean out drawers," Gail responded. I felt insignificant and unproductive. I was sure people would not trade their lives for mine. I was sure Gail preferred her life with a job and an income. I may have been a lady of leisure, but I was poor. I had toyed with the idea of creating a job for myself by going to nearby old folks' homes and offering to teach art or literature classes. In this neighborhood, all of the nursing homes were in stately old buildings or converted mansions; they were not the sterile institutional warehouses we have today. There were three within walking distance of my apartment, so getting to work would not have been hard. But I never pursued it.

Finally, I got the master's degree, and I was ready to teach in college. For the first time, maybe the only time, I asked friends to help me get a job. Jerry and his brother, Davy, had been teaching for several years, Jerry at Bellarmine College, our Catholic college, and Davy at Jefferson Community College. "Tell them I'm your sister!" I was joking, sort of.

It is true what they say about knowing people. Davy had known me for years; we both went to Kentucky Southern College. He knew me as a regular person in a wheelchair. When he got me an interview with Larry Perkins of the English Department at JCC, Larry made me feel he too had known me for years—and he probably did know a lot, because of Davy's friendship. It was a good interview. We discussed possible obstacles and how I would handle them. Since this was a state-run college, it had to comply with federal and local access standards, so the building, while old, was retrofitted with a rebuilt elevator.

I applied to teach night classes, two nights a week for about two hours. I told Larry that, if possible, I wanted to start out with one class. When the interview was over, even though I did not tend to be optimistic, I felt I was finally on my way to a real job: teaching freshman English at a community college.

The next step was to meet with Mr. Hawkins, the college administrator, to fill out employment forms. Mr. Hawkins knew me too; he had worked at Kentucky Southern College. "You will want full time as soon as there is an opening, won't you?" he asked.

Part-time was good, I thought. It would give me plenty of time to prepare for classes, a chance to get used to working, and enough money to feel I had an income of my own. But I was apprehensive about taking on too much. My student-teaching experience with Sister Mary Joseph still hung over me. It contributed to an odd contradictory understanding I held of myself. I did not think I knew any less than any new teacher would, so in that sense, I felt I was as qualified as anyone, disabled or not. But I was, "after all, handicapped," as Sister had said. If she thought it would make me a less qualified teacher, then maybe it would. I did not know for sure, and it made me afraid to try.

I did not recognize that this kind of thinking is the effect of prejudice. I took Sister Mary Joseph's comments to heart and they caused self-doubt. All I knew was that I was about to get my first job, and I was afraid.

I said something to Mr. Hawkins about wanting to do a good job and having to think of my stamina and being in my wheelchair for hours on end. Maybe because he knew me, he was overly helpful. "When you get hired full time," he said, "we can put a chaise longue in your office. That can give you time to rest in between classes. You could even hold student/advisor meetings while you're resting." He made it sound so simple.

As he continued to talk, I kept thinking, How would I do that? Would I get Chris to come in each day to help me out of the chair and onto the chaise longue? Could I hire some students to do it, maybe? But then, could you flunk a student and then expect him to assist you onto a chaise longue? What kind of a relationship would that create with students?

Mr. Hawkins was trying to accommodate me years before any law would even mention the idea. But accepting his accommodation would entail a great deal of arranging—all the asking, organizing backups, hiring people, paying them. I knew I could not handle all the planning a full-time job would take. I was already having trouble finding someone simply to drive me to classes. In fact, the day I signed the contract, I did not yet have a way to get to work.

Since I was going to be teaching evening classes and Chris only worked days, I had to find someone with a car—since I did not own one—who could lift me from my chair into the car and vice versa. Lynda was living with me then. She had a car, but she could not put me in it. I could not tell Mr. Hawkins any of that. I would not want him to think I was incapable. But I was facing an obstacle even bigger than self-doubt.

Transportation is an enormous obstacle to employment for people with disabilities. There was no wheelchair-accessible public transportation in Louisville in the mid-Seventies. I had a lot of friends, but I did not know anyone who had the time or the desire to help me get back and forth to work. Nor should they have to.

Now was one of those times when I envied Franklin Roosevelt. I am sure he never had to worry about how he was going to get to work. I did not have his money or his prestige, so when I called all over town looking for a solution to my transportation need, I was just another crippled person with a problem.

I began with the social service agencies, including Mrs. Scott, the counselor at a family agency whom I had talked to before. She agreed that putting an ad in the newspaper for this kind of job was unwise. She admired my plan to scour the community's resources and had no additional suggestions. So I started calling around.

I found if you have to get to the doctor or therapy or some prearranged charitable social event, the Red Cross would provide transportation. Nothing, however, was available for a wheelchair user trying to get to work. Cabs could take you anywhere, and most drivers would fold your wheelchair and put it in the trunk, but you had to get in and out of the cab yourself. There was no literal *picking up* of passengers.

I tried Vocational Rehabilitation and learned they did not help with transportation. They could help you pay for it until you got your first paycheck, but they could not help find a driver. They could pay for hand controls for your car if you could get yourself in and out of the car and drive. I could not do that.

I called the neighborhood community ministries, who often advertised for senior volunteers to drive people to church and social events. I was expecting to pay. I did not need charity. A secretary answered the phone, wrote down what I needed, and said she would give my message to the director. After two weeks of waiting for the director to call, I called back and learned the lesson of the squeaky wheel. "Yes," he said thoughtfully, "I remember the message. You were going to call me back, weren't you? We don't know of anyone right now. Call me back in a couple of weeks and I'll see if anyone comes to mind."

I had not imagined that finding someone to transport me would be so hard. Since I became disabled as a child, being carried around was no big deal. My brother, M.C., was about fifteen when he carried me up a shale hill from our boat in Lake Cumberland to our car. Once he lifted me out of the boat and started up the shale, he could not stop and change his mind—it was one of those times when you do what you said you would do because people expect you to. The shale was so steep and slippery Daddy had to push M.C. to make sure he did not tumble back down. I was scared because M.C. seemed tense, but I knew I was safe with him.

Chris regularly picked me up and put me in the car. Once I hired a student at Kentucky Southern College to put me in Janet's car so I could take a late afternoon art class and ride home with her. Girlfriends picked me up; so did my boyfriends. Darlene said it was not hard to carry me around. It was somewhat hard to pick me up and set me down sometimes, but once she had me in her arms, she said, she could carry me anywhere. Once for an afternoon tryst, a boyfriend carried me from the car, across the street, up to the front porch, through the front door, and up two flights of stairs to his third-floor apartment. Afterward we went out for a steak dinner. Either he found me irresistible, or he was desperate for a tryst.

So for years it was normal for me to be picked up and carried (until my forties, when my bones begged me to stop). What was not normal was having to talk about it so much. I do not like to talk about what I need. And here I was doing it over and over again: "Hello, my name is Cass Irvin, I-R-V-I-N, and I use a wheelchair and I am about to get a job teaching and I need . . ."

This was much harder than asking someone to push me down the hall to my next class. Part of the difficulty was having to answer the same questions during every call: What about cabs? (Access; cost.) Red Cross? (Already called them.) Colleges, your church? (I did not have a church.) March of Dimes? (Kids, not jobs.) ALPHA?

Everyone asked: Do you know about ALPHA? ALPHA, Inc., was the Action League for Physically Handicapped Adults. The name, I learned, was significant. Action: These people were not going to fool around; they would be proactive and advocacy oriented. League: an association of political entities for a common purpose. Physically: This was not an organization for people with mental retardation; at this time there were no advocacy organizations set up for non-mentally retarded, disabled adults. Handicapped: It was the mid-1970s; disability rights was new, and the movement was active only in California, Texas, Michigan, and New York; "disabled," as a term, was not "in" yet. Adults: the founders of ALPHA, Inc., wanted the community to know that this was not an organization for crippled children; it was made up of disabled adults who were running the organization, deciding the issues. It was the first of its kind in Louisville.

Most of the people who referred me to ALPHA did not know much about the organization, except that it was for handicapped adults. ALPHA gave me a booklet about all the churches that provided transportation and said they wanted to work with other handicapped people on transportation issues. I thought: Not me, not now; I am trying to solve my immediate problem.

So I started calling churches. I left messages with two secretaries, and on my third call a minister answered the phone. We had a little discussion about my needs, with a few questions from him (Have you called ALPHA?) and finally, a few encouraging words. "You know, my dear, I know if God wants you to have this job, He will provide you with a driver." I wanted so badly to reply to him, "He told me to call you," but I did not have the guts.

I guess God did want me to have the job because about that time Michael lost his factory job and found he could stay in his Louisville apartment on very little money—which driving me back and forth to work would help provide. Several families from his hometown, Lebanon, had moved to Louisville, so he had lots of friends to give him food. I hired Michael to be my transportation provider.

Michael drove me to my first night on my first job, teaching one evening class of freshmen English at Jefferson Community College. Not much happens during the first class: people are in and out, looking for the correct classroom; the teacher tells students the class requirements and assignments. I was prepared for every eventuality, including bringing something to read aloud to kill time if my orientation went by too fast.

On the way from my apartment to the community college, less than two miles away, I was scared to death. I cannot bear to explain the degree or depth of my fear, because to remember it makes the feeling come back. "Scared to death," I believe, means you are so scared you think of death as a way out. That evening, on the way to class, I kept thinking: God, please let me die in a car crash and then I will not have to go through this.

I had felt self-conscious, but not scared, when I graduated from college and TV cameras recorded the event. Two wheelchair-using students graduating from one college—Janet and I—were a real news story. Both of us were escorted by our brothers, who lifted us, wheelchairs and all, onto the stage and pushed us across to get our diplomas with bright camera lights flashing in our faces. All four of us were on the six o'clock news.

My student teaching was hard and I was apprehensive part of the time, but not terrified, because I eased into it.

Now, in the car, I could not get my mind off the fear I was feeling. Franklin Roosevelt was right: once I was able to step back—about twenty years later—I realized there is nothing to fear but fear itself. But that fear on the first night of class was paralyzing me. I am not sure why I was so scared. I knew I could do this work. I had made sure not to take on too many classes. Maybe it was pressure—so much effort had gone into getting me to this point. But I could get out of it. I had a good excuse: It would be less work for others if I stayed home. I knew if I did not succeed, my parents would take care of me. I might have to go home to my back bedroom at Mom and Dad's, but I would not be destitute. Of course, without this job I could not have the life I wanted.

Maybe I was scared because it was a real job. All the way down Broadway toward JCC, I screamed silently, "Michael, stop the car!" But I did not open my mouth.

The driving arrangement between Michael and me worked well for one semester. Michael picked me up, put me and my manual wheelchair in his car, and off we went. At the college, he took me to the classroom. The reverse happened after class. I liked being escorted to class by a handsome young guy, although I was sometimes bugged when he picked me up with his friend Sally in the car. Sally's parents and Michael's parents were good friends. Sally was practically family, I liked to tell myself. I did not have a problem with the fact that my relationship with Michael was not monogamous. In those days few relationships were. But, like my mom, I did not want to know about the others.

Then the Christmas holidays came, Michael went home to Lebanon, and his car died. When he came back to Louisville, he would be without a car, so I found myself needing a new driver. Ideally, I wanted a nice older man, retired, physically fit, active, and with time on his hands. And I found him—my dad. I had to admit he had good qualifications and lots of experience. Not only had he taken me to my high school prom and to all of my extracurricular activities in college, he was often my driver for noncollege activities. Once he picked me up after a Peter, Paul, and Mary concert and brought along a buddy, a salesman. Evidently they were a little intoxicated. His friend kept knocking folk music, thinking it funny to ask me, over and over, "I just want to know, did they ever find a goddamn hammer?"

But going to the Bob Dylan concert was the worst. I guess Daddy was in a hurry, because he was not careful as he pushed me through the crowd of exiting concertgoers. He almost ran over the people in front of us. Wheelchair users learn early on that if someone pushing your chair runs it into someone, it is not your fault. It does not help with the embarrassment or feelings of guilt, but it is *not* your fault. I kept asking Daddy to slow down. Walking not four feet in front of us was a tall, lanky guy with long, thick, curly, dark brown Beatle-cut hair. (Those of us with thin mousy hair always notice hair.) He was wearing a short black velvet cape and had two girls hanging on his arms. He was gorgeous. I was instantly in love. "Daddy, slow down. You're going to run into that guy."

He responded loudly, "If I looked like that, I'd want someone to run over me."

So the old retired guy I found to drive me to work was my young retired father When new management came into his firm, Porter Paint, they had wanted to get rid of the old guard. Daddy was not old guard, exactly, but he did not like these young upstarts, nor did they like his reputation as a playboy or his way of burning the candle at both ends. It was easy to get rid of him during this time of transition. I think he took the driving job mainly to save money.

As a driver, Daddy did as good a job as Michael. He did not bring his girlfriends with him, but I think he did meet someone at the college while he was waiting for my class to get out. Having my dad pick me up did not create as great an image as having Michael do it, but Daddy was free.

The two evenings a week we drove back and forth to work gave me the opportunity to get to know my father. I think it started one day when he picked me up with a bourbon on the rocks in the car's drink holder. This was normal for him. It was the Seventies. It had been a particularly tedious day for me, and I said, "Can I have a sip?" From that day on Daddy had a drink waiting for me in the car. On more than one occasion, by the time we drove those two miles from JCC to my apartment, I was looped. Sometimes Michael met us to carry me inside, and he would laugh at me.

I did not need a drink after work. The fear that tried to force me to kill myself on the first day of class was gone after a few weeks of teaching. But I could still be easily intimidated by older students, who, by experience alone, had to be smarter than I. And I knew there were really bright students in my class. One girl, on her first day, glanced up at me with a look that said, Teach me something! I tried to keep ahead of her, and I think I finally won her over because when I did mess up, usually with grammar, I got so flustered that she took pity on me and came to my aid.

I spent extra time on her essays. I believe the time I spent grading my students' papers was the only time I could teach them individually. Davy, who helped me get this teaching job, laughed out loud when I told him I took about an hour and half to grade each paper.

"Cassie, honey," he lectured me, "you're spending way too much time on this. Fifteen minutes, tops! Anything more and you are working too hard." Of course, Davy was working full time; I taught only two classes, two nights a week. He was right, though: If I was ever going to work full time, I would have to teach differently.

After I had lived in my apartment two years, I took an inventory of my life. I was living the way my friends did, except my dad paid part of my expenses. I worked only part-time and I had expenses my friends did not have: I had to pay someone to live with me and their expenses; I could not catch a bus on the corner; every five years or so, I had to buy a new wheelchair.

Because of my stamina, I did not see full-time employment in my future. I had what I needed because my family had enough money to support my independence. But that kind of independence has it own price.

When I looked toward the future, I realized that no matter how hard I worked I could never earn enough money to pay the expenses of living with a disability. And Mother and Daddy could not take care of me forever.

I was beginning to realize that there were obstacles that, even with perseverance, even with great strength and endurance (which I was not sure I had), I was not going to be able to "overcome." When I got out into the world, into my first apartment, I did not consider myself "one of those"—the stigma attached to people with disabilities. Being "poor unfortunates" or "one of those" was everything society saw as negative about being disabled. Disabled people were uneducated either because they did not have the capacity or because they did not try. The "poor unfortunates" came to a museum with a group on a bus, and, once they disembarked, everybody moved away from them. The "poor unfortunate" was the person in church that everyone said extra prayers for and spoke to because it was the polite thing to do.

I never saw myself as "one of those." But I could no longer avoid the realization that things were not turning out very successfully for me, college or no. I was poor. Although I knew perfectly well that I belonged over here with the fortunate, I could no longer avoid noticing that I could just as easily end up over there as a "poor unfortunate." If I didn't mind my Ps and Qs, I was going to be "one of those" myself.

If I had money I could have had it all: a driver whenever I wanted, a motorized wheelchair, more personal assistance. Because I could not earn enough money, did that mean I should not have these things? Did that mean I should not be able to live a real life?

Something had to change, and I was going to have to get more involved in changing that "something." While I was having these feelings and not knowing what to do about them, a friend, Linc, said: "You should meet Mary Johnson. You should talk to her. You would like each other." Linc told me Mary was working with an organization called ALPHA, and they were looking for people for their board of directors. Finally I was going to find out about ALPHA.

When I called Mary the first time, she was what I have come to lovingly call "being so Mary Johnson." She was upstairs in her bedroom. When she picked up the phone, it sounded as though she was straining, then tumbling. She finally said, "Hello!" and I asked if I had called at a bad time. (It sounded like a bad time.)

"No." she assured me. "I just had to straddle the bed to get to the phone. No, it's not a bad time if you don't mind me moving around some. Godfrey! Hush, I can't hear."

She was talking to her cat. She had been painting the bedroom. She said she was hoping to get it done before her husband got home from work. Her phone had an exceptionally long cord so she could walk all over the room and down the hall, which I think she did while we were talking. I asked her what kind of paint was she using. It was a test question: I judge all people by the paint they use.

My father worked for Porter Paint Company for over forty years. He began by cleaning out paint cans during high school, worked there to get himself through college, and then worked in the chemistry labs. He was vice president of traffic, environment, and safety when he retired. As kids, whenever we saw a Porter Paint truck with its cream and orange stripes, Daddy would say, "There goes our bread and butter." It was explained to us that since Daddy worked there, they paid him, and we bought bread and butter with the money. Porter Paint was our bread and butter. My little-girl mind kept thinking of the company's orange-and-cream-striped trucks. I reasoned that the cream color was the butter, so was the bread orange? I didn't want to eat orange bread.

Mary said she was using Porter Paint. "Godfrey! Get out of here! You're going to get cat hair on my fresh paint!" She told me she was on the ALPHA board. The organization was moving from being an all-volunteer group to being a service organization with support staff. ALPHA had a part-time executive director; she was disabled and a cofounder of the organization. They had a small office in an old hospital, St. Joseph's Infirmary, where coincidentally I stayed after I had polio. Most important, ALPHA was beginning to develop real advocacy activities.

Mary talked about disability rights as though they were just like civil rights and women's right to equality. This was new to me, but it made so much sense. Dr. Haak's words came back to me: "You guys should march on Washington." Mary also talked a lot about the media and the disability image. She pointed out how damaging it is to people with disabilities, as it has been for women, to have to battle the media's perception of the proper body image. It was not right that society could say to her, just because she was not 5' 10" and did not have a 36–24-36 figure, that she could not be a model if that was her aspiration.

After nearly an hour on the phone, we decided to get together. Mary was the public relations director for the Kentuckiana Girl

Scout Council, conveniently located on Cherokee Road about three blocks from my apartment. She would come to me. I knew they were looking for board members and thought that Linc had probably said something to Mary like: "I found you a live one! She has an education, is only working part-time, and she's disabled." It was nice to think someone needed me.

More important, what Mary said had moved me. I was affected especially by the talk about body image. Even though I knew from college psych classes that "you can't love others if you don't love yourself," I always reasoned that I loved my inside self but because my body was not straight and did not work very well, I did not have to love it.

On the day I was to meet Mary Johnson, I sat ensconced in bed with the covers neatly folded at the foot, wearing regular clothes, trying not to look much like an invalid but like someone who is productive, someone with an education and a job. In those days, I got in my wheelchair for washing my hair and going to Jefferson Community College, but I spent most of my time in bed. That is one reason I wanted the biggest room in my apartment for my bedroom: If you are there so much of the time, it has to be big. In my room I had my automatic bed, a dresser and chest of drawers, and bookshelves made from plywood boards and spools covered in jute. In front of the bookshelves was a fainting couch my landlady rented to me, and by the door leading to the living room, I had my TV and TV stand and stereo record player.

From my bed, I could easily see through the living room to the front door. Since it was late afternoon, we had not turned the lights on, so it was fairly dark except for the daylight coming through the front windows. The twelve-foot ceilings and big glass windows made my living room seem cavernous. Lynda answered the door. I recognized Mary's voice immediately, but it was dark and I could not see her.

I could hear Mary talking to Lynda about having lived nearby on Edenside Drive before buying her house in Crescent Hill. They chatted as Lynda directed her toward my room. Soon, standing in my bedroom doorway, framed by the dark living room behind her (which may have distorted my vision), stood a tiny sparkling-bright person.

She was short, yet she filled the room. She had a full head of thick dark-brown hair cropped short. She wore a bright orange, green, and yellow horizontally zigzag-striped sleeveless A-line sundress, cinched at the waist with a wide white belt, and bright green and yellow sandals with no stockings; she carried a brief-case and a white plastic totebag purse with big red flowers on it. Yep, Mary was right, no one would call her "model material." I liked her immediately.

Her energy and enthusiasm was enticing. The more I talked to her, the more I wanted to become involved in trying to change things. I had assets they needed: time and an education. And I had experience living life with a disability.

I was able to make this kind of commitment because Michael was there to take most of the physical barriers away. It was that September that Lynda moved out and Michael became my atten-dant. I am sure I would not have gotten so involved with disabil-ity rights if she had stayed, for it meant going to more meetings, maybe even out of town. Lynda could not do the things for me that Michael could do.

I think Mary and I clicked because she had the vision and I had a sense of order. When I became involved with ALPHA, it had a small United Way grant as start-up money but needed to get better organized and serious about board setup and responsibil-ity. Since board training was provided, I felt pretty confident that I could be a good board member. All my life I doubted my intel-ligence, but I always knew I could learn.

One of my first lessons, not taught in any workshop, was that the people who come together to work on a common cause do so for different reasons. Some come because the issue is important to them and affects their lives; some, because the person or peo-ple initiating the activity is important to them; some, because it affects their job or career. Quite often, the former group does not have the knowledge to make change, the latter group has too little passion about the issue to make change, and the people in the middle are doing someone a favor—too often, they do not want to take real responsibility for an organization. I came to ALPHA because disability issues wcrc important to me every day of my life, and I was ready to take some responsibility for change.

In January 1976 I was elected to the board of directors of ALPHA, Inc., where I served as secretary of the board, chair of the Ways and Means Committee, member of the ad hoc Reorganization Committee, and member of the ad hoc Nominating Committee. ALPHA had money for staff but no supervisor. Since I only taught part-time and lived so close to the office, I also offered to serve as staff liaison/office manager.

I met George Zocklein, another person with vision, through my work with ALPHA. His vision was about developing resources so community and social change organizations could have the funds they need to carry out their programming. He was the kind of person who woke up in the middle of the night thinking of grant ideas, new resources, programs that could get funded—right out of *Rules for Radicals*, Saul Alinsky's 1971 book on how to effect constructive social change. Alinsky outlined rules for organizers to follow in bringing together people for social and political justice. Some people considered it a primer for hell-raisers. George could be that as well, and I learned a lot about community organizing from him. But mostly George taught me about grants.

If you get involved with nonprofits and they find out you are an English major, they assume you can write—at least a complete sentence—and they think you like to write, so they immediately think: grants. In those days, grantsmanship was a new career opportunity. If an organization cannot pay you to write the grant, the idea was to write yourself into the grant as a budget item. So I decided to add grant writing to my resume and set out to educate myself about grantsmanship. I took a class at the University of Louisville's Institute for Community Development but soon discovered that George had already taught me more.

When I became a member of ALPHA's board, I joined with only one stipulation: I would not be active with the general membership. I did not want to associate with disabled people. This is hard to admit, and I am embarrassed by my feelings but I had always been told by my family that I was not like other "handicapped" people. I bought into society's stigma about people with disabilities. I had seen the kids on the telethons, in ugly brown shoes and braces. People felt sorry for them. My mom told me I was not like those kids and, even though I wore the same brown shoes and braces, I believed her.

Society had taught me that disabled people were to be looked down upon. They did not get out much, so they did not have very good manners (possibly because they did not get out much). And, since most of them were not well educated, they were poor.

Poor of itself was not bad; my dad had grown up poor. You could be poor but hardworking and proud. Poor was not of itself good, but you could still take care of yourself, keep yourself clean, Mom would say. But disabled people are helpless; they need to be taken care of. They are burdens; they are of little or no value—except as inspirations. But "disabled people" was me; If I thought disabled people had no value, then I had no value—no matter how much I overcame.

About that time, I met Beth, an ALPHA member who was a new board member, along with me. She wore hippie clothes, long skirts like I did— except her skirt never matched her blouse, and her blouse was not always clean. She wore bedroom slippers in public and she always had dirty hair. She was the kind of person my mom said I was *not* like. Beth was "one of those."

Later I learned Beth was married, and not to someone who could help her wash her hair. That made me think of Mom, who tried to take care of me but could not do it very well, so she hired a maid to help her. I never had dirty hair when Chris took care of me. Without a paid personal assistant, I would have had dirty hair, too. It was not Beth's fault that she had dirty hair; she simply did not have the resources she needed.

Working with ALPHA to change life for people with disabilities was easier than asking for help for myself. If I could be a part of making change for disabled people, then things would change for me, too. It was easier to be political than it was to be personal.

But it was hard work. Besides being a board member, I became a community representative. One of the cornerstones of President Johnson's War on Poverty was the notion of having disadvantaged citizens serve as watchdogs over government programs. And people with disabilities were benefiting from this policy because we were asked to be involved. Simply put, we are the best authority on our lives and needs.

One of my responsibilities was to attend the meetings of the Louisville and Jefferson County Human Relations Commission's Education Committee. As a community representative, I was to address educational issues that affected disabled students and present the issues to the committee. I probably was a token, but I was happy to have my foot in the door, so to speak.

I learned so much about discrimination and civil rights. I learned that civil rights movements occur because human beings do not treat each other fairly. I learned that people can come together on an issue and go as far as they must to solve the problem.

The Education Committee noticed that a disproportionate number of black students with behavioral problems were being put in public school special ed classes as a form of discipline. Was this an epidemic, or was it educational discrimination? As the committee studied the issue, people came together; a parents' group evolved into SPARC, the Student Parent Advocacy Resource Center; and real change began to happen for those students.

I took my job as disability representative seriously and became knowledgeable on disability education issues. As a member of ALPHA, I was asked to report to the committee concerning the Education of All Handicapped Children Act, P.L. 94–142. I put together handouts for the group. In my report I outlined the law, discussed the segregation of children in special schools, and talked about parents' desires for the integration of their disabled kids. I enjoyed prepping for the presentation because it was teaching again.

Before I gave my report, I was sitting next to Dr. Lyman Johnson in the boardroom of the Human Relations Commission. I did not know who he was, but I noticed that people treated him differently. They were very respectful, patient, almost reverent. Later I learned that he had been a leader in the civil rights movement in Kentucky. In the 1930s, he taught history at the segregated Central High School in Louisville, where he organized black teachers to protest their salaries—15 percent lower than those of white teachers; they sued and they won. He led battles to integrate the city's restaurants, theaters, swimming pools, and hotels. Many of his high school students joined him, sitting in at lunch counters and picketing downtown hotels. And he broke the color barrier at the University of Kentucky, attending classes even while crosses burned on campus. In 1979, the university invited him back to receive an honorary Doctor of Letters degree.

When I met Lyman Johnson, thirty years after he organized sit-ins, he was an old, thin, gangly, shriveled, handsome and impeccably dressed man in his dark pin-striped suit, a bright handkerchief in his coat pocket, white shirt, vest, tie, and shiny black shoes. His wife was ill. You could tell by the way he talked about her that she was very important to him. She was in a nursing home and he had become resigned to it. He was beginning to have some mobility problems himself.

When my presentation was over and the committee took a break, the elderly civil rights leader, courtly and courteous, began talking to me. He said I had done a good job of explaining the law. He was familiar with it, he said, but told me he had learned something from my talk—and that he agreed with me in principle. "Now you know it is going to cost a whole lot of money," he added. "I wonder if it might just too expensive to put ramps everywhere."

I simply looked at him. Here was a man who had been in the forefront of the civil rights movement, who had seen the harm that segregation and isolation in inferior schools had caused African American children. But it might be "too expensive to put ramps everywhere."

I found it difficult to respond. I wanted to be respectful, since I was a new committee member. I did not want to offend. But I screwed up my courage and said, "You never would have accepted that as an argument to halt busing for desegregation." He smiled, and I watched him as he began to formulate an answer. Then someone tapped him on the shoulder. He turned away and the moment was lost. Lyman Johnson never answered me.

Evidently I did a good job with my presentation. Later I heard that Jim Rosenblum, a commissioner and Education Committee member, left that meeting and went to visit the mayor, suggesting to him that I be appointed to the Human Relations Commission. And I was.

From that moment on, I knew what I was here for.

ALPHA was like many new organizations. So much needs to be done that the organization takes on too many responsibilities. The result is the group becomes fractured and almost ineffectual. As much as we tried to manage well, to build a stable organization, we found this happening in ALPHA. One faction on the board wanted ALPHA to take action right now against inaccessible buildings and sue people. Sadly, the majority of the board did not care one way or another. So there was conflict.

One day Jim Cherry appeared at my office, the same Jim Cherry whose future lawsuit, *Cherry v. Matthews*, would force the signing of the Rehabilitation Act's Section 504 regulations. Jim was formidable in both stature and reputation.

"Stop!" he ordered his attendant, who brought his wheelchair to a halt in the office doorway. Jim had been on the ALPHA Board since the beginning. Although he had been hospitalized often in Maryland, no one seemed to know why he was disabled—including his doctors. Jim was one of the people who taught me that the cause of your disability does not really matter. What matters is what you can do, or what you want to do; the rest can always be worked out.

Jim accomplished a lot for a man whose doctors claimed he should have died from his disability. He was strong, ramrod straight, and tall in his manual wheelchair. He did not come into the office; it was too small for two wheelchairs. "You know, all this board organizing and training is a waste of time," he began. "We need to be doing something like filing lawsuits." Jim had created a guerrilla handbook to teach people how to file suit against owners of inaccessible buildings. I knew he was not just a big talker; he was a doer.

And I knew Jim was right in his aggressive attitude. Someone needed to do the work he was doing. But I felt that ALPHA should get stable first. We were on notice from our major funding source that we needed a better educated, more responsible board of directors. I thought we should tend to this before exerting our energies on something else. We did not want to lose our funding, our staff. I said so in the nicest way.

Jim bit my head off. My experience has always been that when people get loud, they are angry. Jim seemed very angry, and I was uncomfortable sitting in this little office listening to him sputter about how wrong we were. "We don't need money. We need action!" I kept thinking, well, you do need money—for paper and phones and typewriters and such—to be able to take action. At that moment I realized we were both right. He was just louder than I was.

Soon afterward, several of us on ALPHA's board—including Mary, Beverly Merschede, and Ann Tafel, and me—exhausted from the squabbling, decided to use our energy to build a new organization. We wanted something different than advocacy or services, so we decided to create a research and consulting organization that focused on disability rights issues. We would be a nonprofit collective organization, with volunteer board members taking direct responsibility for projects. We called the organization Prime Movers, Inc. (PMI).

A minor quake ensued in the Louisville disability community when we formed. There were already all kinds of groups for people with visual disabilities, people with mental disabilities, and, of course, crippled kids. There were all kinds of women's organizations. But starting a new disability organization was considered detrimental. We became known as "the splinter group" and had to work extra hard to prove ourselves.

We thought if we could talk to the prime movers in the community—the county judge, the mayor, the planners, the shakers—we could persuade them to see the importance of making our community accessible. If we could explain the necessity of it, the moral rightness of access, why, they would just do it.

Perhaps this idea was naive, but we believed it. We searched for people who had the same dream. George used to say: "Either get a board that believes in and works hard to achieve the goals of the organization, or get a turkey board of people who trust your vision and will let you do what you need to do." We looked for the former and we found them: George and my brother, M.C., who both advised us; and Charlie and Sara Pratt, who served as board members. The Pratts had just moved to Louisville; he worked for city government and she was an attorney. We began to educate people. It was the late 1970s.

Mary Johnson made a presentation to the committee set up to plan the new Kentucky Center for the Arts, chaired by Barry Bingham Sr., the publisher of our two city newspapers and an important arts contributor. The committee took her suggestions about universal design to heart, and today the arts center reflects them. Actor's Theatre of Louisville began disability awareness sessions after PMI board members Sara and Charlie Pratt did sensitivity training for their staff.

But the best thing PMI did in the early days, I think, was help organize a coalition of disability groups to push the county judge and mayor to do a demographic study of disabled residents in our county. We were tired of people saying things like: "How do we know inaccessibility is a big problem? There aren't that many of you out there, are there? We never see you out there."

Our coalition, the Alliance for Disability Demographics Studies (ADDS), lobbied for the disability study, pushing county officials to survey the population to discover our numbers and needs. We felt it would help the whole community with program planning and would ensure that disability programs got their share of community resources.

The name ADDS was important. We wanted people to know we were together on this issue of a demographic study. We felt the term "alliance" made the member groups feel equal (we were having territorial problems). PMI's role in the coalition was to get information to the members and to handle the gofering of letters, petitions, position statements, and final proposal with everyone's signatures. Accessible transportation was practically nonexistent. There were no faxes, no e-mail, no talking computers. To save time we read everything to everybody.

Our lobbying was successful. In 1979, the county hired a research firm, Consensus, Inc., to do the demographic and needs assessment study, one of the first of its kind in the country. The results, released in 1980, showed that eighty thousand people in Jefferson County had disabilities—twice as many as had been thought. Because of the data, government officials had to recognize this segment of the population and begin addressing our needs. The city funded the Kentuckiana Radio Readers Service for people with visual disabilities and a housing program for disabled people as a result.

By now, PMI had a good reputation. We did advocacy activities as individuals and educational projects as an organization. Because of our association with George Zocklein, who by now worked for VISTA in Kentucky, we were able to participate in this federal program, touted as "the domestic Peace Corps" (now AmeriCorps *VISTA).

Beginning in the mid-1960s, VISTA volunteers were placed with community-based agencies to find long-term solutions to the problems caused by urban and rural poverty. You could become a VISTA volunteer no matter your age. It was a one-year commitment with a stipend at poverty level, just enough to cover basic living expenses.

Volunteers ran the gamut from socially conscious college students not sure yet what they wanted to do in life to retirees who had already done it all and now did it for others. Teachers, lawyers, doctors, and architects joined VISTA, like the retired teacher and her retired carpenter husband who both worked in Northern Kentucky in an inner-city community center. Mothers on welfare and people with disabilities signed up. I became a VISTA volunteer, too—for PMI.

The idea of VISTA was conceived by President John F. Kennedy and Attorney General Robert F. Kennedy soon after the Peace Corps was created. It became part of the 1964 Economic Opportunity Act—the War on Poverty legislation of the Johnson administration. VISTA's goal was to eliminate "poverty in the midst of plenty" by offering everyone "the opportunity to work and the opportunity to live in decency and dignity." President Johnson welcomed the first group of VISTA volunteers to the White House in December 1964. According to the AmeriCorps *VISTA Thirtieth Anniversary Booklet, he told them: "Your pay will be low; the conditions of your labor often will be difficult. But you will have the satisfaction of leading a great national effort and you will have the ultimate reward which comes to those who serve their fellow man."[1]

VISTAs were placed all over the United States—in the urban neighborhoods of Hartford, Connecticut; the rural hills of Ken-

---

1. The booklet is available at http://www.friends ofvista.org/living/hist.html (accessed July 2003).

tucky; and the migrant camps of California. They worked in daycare centers in migrant communities, in adult education programs in inner cities, on Native American reservations, and in isolated regions of Alaska.

The program was not without controversy. VISTA volunteers working with coal miners in rural Appalachia were falsely charged with sedition by local authorities. The result was that VISTAs were prohibited from any activity that could be interpreted as political involvement, a ruling that may have helped PMI, because VISTA in Kentucky was very careful where they placed people. To most people, our organization appeared rather benign, so VISTA gave us a good number of volunteers. We were ecstatic. The volunteers gave PMI paid staff; VISTA gave our disability rights movement a lot of strength.

And VISTA gave me training—and a job. VISTA taught its volunteers to evaluate community problems; for example, was there a need for a neighborhood after-school tutoring program? We were also taught how to develop programs; how to write grants, raise funds, or find other resources to pay for them; and how to implement the programs. As VISTAs, we learned about legal aid, tenants' unions, neighborhood organizations, spouse-abuse centers.

I learned that after-school programs in the inner city are not always created for poor black kids. A neighborhood center in Northern Kentucky had organized an after-school program for kids from rural areas whose parents had moved to the big city for jobs and found the environment and culture foreign to them. I learned that rural poor people had a lot to overcome themselves.

VISTA gave me an environment in which to grow and a new sense of myself. Because of the training, I felt qualified. Because of my new awareness, I became more socially conscious. The job was perfect for me: I wanted to be a community organizer. I had been involved enough with disability issues, had enough experience with the community, and was a part of the community we served. Here my experiences counted. I bought the theory that "if you are not part of the solution, you are part of the problem." I wanted to get people more involved with disability. And I was teaching again—just a different subject.

Mary Johnson and I gave a presentation on disability laws and access issues at a VISTA training. Since organizations getting VISTAs were from all over the state, the training was held in a somewhat central location, the Natural Bridge State Park Lodge. The state park system was proud of its newly built conference center nestled in the woods on a mountainside and had tried hard to make the natural setting accessible, with sidewalks and paths everywhere. Except for the tiny step onto their private balconies, the rooms of Hemlock Lodge were pretty accessible.

Being with these people for several days of orientation and training made them feel like friends. I was comfortable talking to friends, but I was nervous about speaking about disability laws. I am not good with facts about legal issues. I felt I was an authority on disability itself, and great at relating life experiences to illustrate why the laws were needed, so I talked about Sister Mary Joseph.

I was elated to be teaching again, but my elation died after we finished our presentation and I realized we had to head down the long, steep hill to the lodge for lunch. The sidewalk was so new that the dirt had not filled in around it, so there was no natural curbing. Usually I like to amaze people with how fast and well I can move about using my motorized wheelchair. But even though my chair had drive belts so it could not run away with me, I was petrified of the hill and the lack of edges on the sidewalk. If I went off, my chair would tip over on top of me, creating a huge spectacle and probably broken bones.

"I'll walk in front of you," Mary offered.

"No," I said. "Walk behind me and *hold on*. If I go toward the edge, pull me back!"

The ride down the hill was bumpy. I wanted to go slowly, but if I didn't keep the joystick pressed forward, the brakes would grab, jerk, and stop me. People were walking all around us, oblivious to our adventure. "Watch out! Coming through!" I called out to them, and they jumped out of the way.

I was acting a little too excited, being silly, but I liked the attention. By now almost everyone was conscious of our adventure. It was a good opportunity for a lesson in the reality of access. Because of its steepness and length, the sidewalk should have had a level place to stop and rest. It could have had curbed edges, too, which would have made it safer. But that was not required by law.

At the bottom, after a big sigh of relief and a thank you to everyone who had walked with us in case the wheelchair went off the sidewalk, I headed into the dining room with the others for lunch. Eileen, one of the people who had trooped down the hill with me, came over to the table where Mary and I were eating. I had liked her from the moment I saw her. She was from New York and had been assigned to a spouse-abuse center in northern Kentucky. She was cool, a hippie folksinger type in a sweatshirt, ragged blue jeans, and a blue bandanna around her curly black hair. (I would die for her hair.)

She complimented us on our workshop. The summer before, she told us, she had worked at a hospital as a medical clerk. What she had experienced there made her see the need for patients to have an advocate to make sure they got what they needed. She realized there needed to be a patient's bill of rights to protect sick people.

"But I never thought about disability civil rights until I heard you guys speak," she went on. As socially conscious as she thought she was, she had never thought of disabled people as having problems with rights. She seemed somewhat embarrassed to admit it. She wanted more information, she said. She promised to stay in touch. She was like many of the people I had known in college, but more socially conscious than I remember being at her age.

Several weeks after that training, the state VISTA director

asked if we were interested in getting another VISTA volunteer. We had originally requested two, including me, but not enough people had signed up that year so there were not enough VISTAs to fill all Kentucky's slots. Eileen was having problems with her supervisor at the spouse-abuse center in northern Kentucky and had come down to check out Louisville's VISTA groups: Legal Aid, the Tenant's Union, and Prime Movers, Inc. She wanted to work with us.

I had my own epiphany during the VISTA training, along with Eileen. Mine came in a workshop on spouse abuse. I had not grown up around abusive situations, but I was not naive about them. Mom and Daddy fought, shouted, and once in a while threw things. Daddy told me that Mom had once thrown his luggage out the door, telling him to leave. But she was drinking at the time, so he did not want to stay anyway, he said.

In the workshop, I could not understand why these abused women did not just get away from the abuse, since they could walk. Just grab your kids and walk away, I thought. You can walk away; I could not. You can get to the spouse-abuse center if you needed to; I could not.

The workshop taught me that many things can paralyze a person other than disease or accident. I knew what psychological abuse was. Mom and Daddy abused each other that way. If he had not taught mother how to drink, my maternal grandmother claimed, she never would have become an alcoholic. If she drank too much and became incapacitated, he had an excuse to leave her for other women. Typical for the upper middle class in the 1960s. If Daddy was ruining Mother's life, why did she not just walk away?

Listening to that workshop presentation, I felt an overwhelming sadness. I had to fight back tears as I realized that I had been abused. I was dependent, and because I was dependent, I was not always in charge of myself, and things happened to hurt me. Of course, it was not like the pain of spousal abuse—but the fear of pain, the fear of having pain inflicted on you, was the same. That fear thing again.

At Warm Springs, I feared being hurt during physical therapy. I tried to warn various therapists over the years not to push my foot or knee or hip too far. "No," they would assure me, "I won't pop it. Just a little more, a little more." CRUNCH!

"Ow!"

"Sorry. Did I push too hard?" People hurt you and then tell you it is for your own good.

When I was little and got carried around, I got bumped and bruised. Daddy used to carry me from the car in the lower-level garage upstairs to my bedroom. Because I wore long leg braces that bent at the knees, my feet stuck out. Often my foot would get bumped coming through the door at the top of the stairs. I would holler, "Ow!" to which Daddy would reply: "It was an accident. You know I didn't do it on purpose!" He would feel bad, and I would feel bad and swear to myself that I would not holler next time so he would not feel bad. Somehow, when you know the pain is coming, it is so much worse.

I think any dependent relationship has the potential for abuse. Mom was not abusive, but I learned not to ask for much. I did not go to the bathroom as often as I should have. Close personal working relationships like that have a tension all their own.

Listening to the women from the spouse-abuse center talk about their experiences, I realized that my present living situation was close to abusive, although I could never say that out loud. Even though Michael was the first person who let me be the most I could be, when he got overtired from the responsibility of me, or from his stereotypical musician's lifestyle of too much drink and too late nights, he would blow up. I was not alarmed. My sister's husband was known for his temper, too, although I had never seen it. I was learning how different people exhibit anger. Some holler and throw things. So if Michael blew up once in a while, I could accept that.

But Michael never understood how the *noise* of anger bothered me. All my life I have been conscious of sounds. Knowing what was happening around me, I thought, kept me safe. When I was little in the house alone with Mom, I had to listen to see if she was sleeping or up. If she was up and had been drinking, I had to listen to see if she was okay. If I heard her fall, I had to listen to make sure she had not hurt herself. If she hurt herself more than a bump or a bruise, I called Daddy at work to ask him to come home and help her. I seldom had to call him, but I always had to listen.

It is hard to listen when there is too much noise. Michael would come home and turn on the music—*loud*. Sometimes there was screaming and yelling, banging and crashing things, as well. It took time for me to figure out if the shouting was for anger or joy. (He was loud when he was happy, too.) It took time to figure out if the screaming was at me or about some apartment complex being built on a nearby farm. I could take the loud music, the stomping around the house, the slamming doors, the singing loudly, the drumming and banging on things. But the noises made me feel like jelly until I could decipher his mood.

At that workshop I realized I was in a dependent situation, just like those women from the spouse-abuse center. I had been in that position all of my life and I always would be. Like many women, I thought it was better to stay with the abuser than to leave him. Michael and I were better together than we were apart. But, listening to those women, I began to realize I might be accepting too much. What could I do? I could not just get up and walk away. I did not have options like a spouse-abuse center to go to. They were inaccessible.

I think Michael sensed that these three days of training had a profound effect on me. When we left the lodge heading home, he and I drove around the Red River Gorge State Park.

We stopped at a lookout point and, without warning, he picked me up out of our car, stepped over the stone wall that said, "Don't go beyond this point!" and sat down on the ground with me in his lap overlooking a gorge. Michael had grown up in this kind of country. He was used to sitting on the sides of mountains.

We watched the sky change colors as the sun went down. It turned a little cool, but we did not move. I began worrying about how was Michael going to stand back up with me in his arms. He would have to lean forward to rise to a standing position, and we were on the side of a mountain. Far down the gorge at our feet, you could see the tops of pine trees. They had to be at least fifty feet tall. How far down was it? If we slipped and fell, we would fall a long time.

I have no sense of physical perspective. I had never been on the side of a mountain before. As a child, I never wanted to do daring things. It was getting really chilly. "Shouldn't we be going?" I asked Michael. He answered, "*Are* we going?" Which meant: If we should be going, we would be going—but we weren't, were we?

"Look!" he said, and pointed into the gorge.

"What?" I gasped. A mist—no, thicker than a mist, more like smoke, with a sweet, wet smell—came wafting up from the ravine toward our feet.

"It's clouds," Michael said. "Now we can go."

We at PMI were happy to have Eileen come work with us. Everyone pitched in to help her find housing and introduce her to our friends. I took her under my wing and even warned her about marihuana. "I don't know if you do or don't—and I'm not asking," I told her. "But if ever you decide to do it, please let me know, because I know safe people. Kentucky doesn't need any more busted VISTAs."

The next year, Eileen and I both re-upped. Before too long, three more VISTAs—Rebecca, Joe, and Tim—transferred from other organizations and came to work for us, more than doubling our staff. Eileen, the mother hen to this group, said to them right off, "If you need *anything*, just go to Cass!"

Some of our VISTAs clearly had disabilities, but we soon learned they did not categorize themselves as disabled. We never discussed it with them. We simply worked to create a climate in which no disabled person seemed to be "one of those"; all were seen simply as people beset by a society filled with discrimination. In the process, a sense of pride developed of its own accord among our VISTAs. They did great deeds (and still do) and wrote articles about disability pride and activism for *The Disability Rag*.

Our VISTAs gave PMI a broader outreach. On their own, they got involved with the Tenants Union, Legal Aid, the Human Relations Commission, the Kentucky Commission on Human Rights, art, ecology, life. Wherever they went, disability consciousness traveled with them. They were good for me, too, because their energy and enthusiasm made me more active. I wanted to be a good role model, a good teacher.

It was Rebecca who maneuvered me into giving my first speech. She was interested in women's issues and got involved with the planning committee for Women's Equality Day observations. Congress in 1971 had instituted this day to honor women's continuing efforts toward equality. All over the country, women's groups rallied to celebrate all kinds of accomplishments of women. When the committee discussed speakers for the 1981 celebration in Louisville, Rebecca volunteered me to speak about disabled women. When she informed me that they wanted me, I felt I could not refuse.

It was a big responsibility. I had not been much involved with women's issues beyond consciousness-raising groups. I read *The Feminine Mystique* years after it was published, when I was living in the country and kind of isolated. Betty Friedan's words struck home; I was searching for comparisons, and I found my life in those pages.

Everyone wants value as a person. This was what Betty Friedan saw when women faced the "problem that has no name"—the sense that part of themselves was being denied. Disabled people want this same value, but we still feel we have to hide our need for help and accommodation because it is not yet considered normal. We can't be happy about ourselves for just being ourselves. When people say, "I don't consider you disabled," and we view it as a compliment, we do not see that we have denied a part of ourselves. As with women, the freedom to make choices, to make decisions on our own for our own lives, is missing.

The Feminine Mystique and the women's movement helped women realize that they should make choices, not let society dictate what they will be, what roles they must choose. I wondered what the world would be like if disabled people were given choices.

Feminism is a philosophy, a way of looking at life, a way of being. It is accepting and nurturing. It is sisterhood. It is the feeling of camaraderie I felt when I spoke at Women's Equality Day in 1981. And I have tried desperately to share it with my disabled sisters and brothers because that feeling continues to be empowering.

Like women, most disabled people I know still seem to regard their problems as the result of their disabilities rather than of discrimination. In their heart of hearts they might know that discrimination is the culprit, but they never say so. Each seems to view his or her own situation, if not as unique, certainly as not the common situation of disabled people nationwide. Too often, they seem to give the matter no real thought. If I do not have an attendant, that may seem to be my personal problem. But when twenty-five of us need attendants, when thousands of us across the state, or millions of us nationwide, need them and cannot afford them, that is no longer just my personal problem. It is an issue—a social issue.

When society thinks of "disabled people" as a group, we are not viewed as members of an oppressed group pushing for dignity as humans or for rights. We are never thought of, even by those who consider themselves liberal, in the same terms as gays or African Americans. We are simply "the handicapped" or "the disabled." Poor, hopeless unfortunates. No wonder FDR called himself a "cured cripple." He did not want to be a part of the group society saw as helpless. Most disabled people instinctively want to pass rather than be identified as "one of those."

Roosevelt's message—that you cannot let them see how disabled you are not if you expect to succeed—is the message today's "successful" disabled person has internalized. This belief has kept most of us from joining activist groups to change society. Roosevelt did not seem to know how to change society so that it did not care if he were in a wheelchair or not. We do not seem to know how today, either.

I believe that the feminization of the disability rights movement—applying the tenets of the feminist movement to this other minority, people with disabilities—has to happen before we can truly succeed as a movement, as a people. That is why my goal on that Women's Equality Day in 1981 was to say something that would bring women into our movement. With the help of women's groups, I knew we could do more to change things.

Preparing the speech made me realize that this was what had been missing from my life and my work in the movement: sisterhood. This was another thing society had taken from me. I needed that sense of strength that sisterhood brings. Psychologist Carol Gill said disabled people resist coming together because of the social stigma. When I prepped for that speech, I realized I had some responsibility to overcome the stigma myself. I had to find that camaraderie for myself among my people. And once I did, I would no longer be alone.

Michael dropped me off at Sixth and Main Streets the day I gave my speech. I made my way up the ramped walkway to Belvedere Park overlooking the Ohio River. I was on my own; Rebecca would meet me here. All over the sunny park were booths from women's groups, people of all ages and all colors, mostly women and children. Food carts and children's activities kept people occupied until the formal celebration began. The whole park smelled like cotton candy and suntan lotion.

At the far end of Belvedere Park, a speaker's platform had been set up. Rebecca was waiting nearby and showed me the ramp to the platform, too steep, of course, but she assured me someone would walk behind me. There was a podium on the platform, but, since I do not stand, I was not going to use it. I was to sit beside the podium when it was my turn. That meant I was going to have to read my speech from papers in my lap. I was scared but excited. That day, I told the crowd:

I am very happy to be here. As I look around me and I feel the atmosphere that surrounds all of us here, I am amazed. I have never experienced the love, the strength, the sense of sisterhood and group power and confidence that I feel here. I only wish that more of my disabled sisters could be here to experience this, too.

There is a commercial on television. It shows a little baby, a cute baby, and the narrator says: "This child was born with a handicap. She was born female." I guess that means I have been twice cursed.

We are celebrating today the accomplishments of women. Because I am disabled and I have been involved with the disability rights movement, I am supposed to focus on the accomplishments of Kentucky's disabled women. But, I must confess that I know very little that has been accomplished. I am not saying that we haven't had successes, but I am saying that I believe that successful disabled women in Kentucky do not identify themselves as such.

And why should they?

Disability does not yet have the positive connotations that sisterhood does. While today many people are proud to be feminists, no one that I know of is proud to be identified as disabled and a part of the disability rights movement.

Our society believes that a woman with one leg can't be a doctor; a woman who can't see can't run a store; a woman who can't hear can't be a supervisor; a woman in a wheelchair can't be a lawyer. Are those truly misconceptions? you may be asking yourself. Yes, they are. They are just like the misconceptions our society had about women fifty years ago.

Overcoming society's misconceptions is hard. That is one problem disabled and nondisabled women have in common. We have many other problems in common. But I believe that disabled women do not recognize this commonality. Because of that, the achievements in the women's movement—to disabled women—would not seem to be relevant. Thus, they are not active in your rights movement.

I have been involved with disability rights for about seven years, but it was only recently that I first began to see the relevancy of the women's movement in my life. It happened when I read *The Feminine Mystique*. I did not read it to learn more about myself as a woman. I read it to learn more about other disadvantaged people and to learn how to better approach the problems of my people, disabled people.

Actually, I was looking for a formula for getting my people more involved in their fight for their own rights. I couldn't figure out why more disabled people didn't get involved.

Incidentally, I found that disabled people were too busy just trying to live a life with all the obstacles they have to confront. They were just too busy getting by. That's when I discovered that the women who began the fight for rights were middle-class women—women who had the education and the time.

When I read *The Feminine Mystique* I made three observations:

First—there were a lot of boring and complicated statistics and charts and data in the book.

Second—much of what I was reading was not earth shattering. In fact, it was rather passé. Of course, I had to remember that I was reading the book about fifteen years after it had been published.

Third—the observation that really shocked me, in the book all you had to do was change one word (or really add one word) and you were talking about disabled women—and you were talking about disabled women today.

Disabled women today are like the women in *The Feminine Mystique*! We are the women who seem to be filling our lives with meaningful/ meaningless tasks—and wondering why we have a strange sensation of loss. We are the ones who take all day to clean one room of a house. We are the ones who are accepting society's view of what we should be instead of deciding what it is we want to be.

Your disabled sisters are still the women of the feminine mystique. We are the women who are living the lives society has dictated for us. And we are beginning, just beginning, to realize that perhaps that's not the role for us. We are just beginning to feel that we should be getting a little more from life. We are just beginning to wonder why we are not feeling those feelings of fulfillment and satisfaction we see on the faces of our nondisabled sisters. We are just beginning to listen when nondisabled sisters talk about their fight, the struggles, the accomplishments, and we are beginning to wonder when we are going to feel that way. We are just beginning to wonder if perhaps society could be wrong in its view of disabled women and their abilities.

But it's hard to ignore what society thinks. Disabled woman have not accomplished much because they are not yet strong enough to disregard what society tells them about themselves. It is hard to be a woman and sit in a room with men and feel equal—especially when they say, "Yes, honey, what was it you wanted to say?" It is very hard to sit in a wheelchair in a roomful of nondisabled women and feel that you are equal, especially when they say to you, "Yes, dear, what was it you wanted to say?"

It is hard for disabled women to feel a pride in themselves and feel they have anything to celebrate. And to get involved in any rights movement, my disabled sisters have to be aided, just as other minority women have had to be assisted to come into the mainstream of the women's movement.

It was not easy to convince women, who after thirty years of marriage found themselves on their own, that a liberation movement was for them. It wasn't easy to convince economically disadvantaged women that this kind of involvement was for them. It has been hard work trying to get these women convinced. But it has been worth it to have these women involved.

I agree that nondisabled women should assist disabled women to get involved with the fight to assure equality of all people. But I am beginning to believe that until groups coalesce, it does not much matter what we do or what we say. Working together, we can accomplish much. Our voices can be strong—even when we use interpreters.

Thank you.

By the time I finished, my papers were scattered on the platform around me. There was applause, but I was too concerned to enjoy it, backing down the too-steep ramp and getting off the platform so the next speaker could take my place. Someone helped me down the ramp, and another person gathered up my papers and handed them to me as I made my way from the speaker platform and through the crowd. All the way along, people patted me on the shoulder or shook my hand. "Congratulations!" "Good job!"

I moved away from the open spaces. I had been in the sun for about two hours, and even though I used suntan lotion on my face and hands daily, I was concerned I would get a bad sunburn. I sat in the columned walkway on the Belvedere to listen to the last speaker, Allie Hixon. She was a well-known leader for women in Kentucky. I had been in meetings with her but had never heard her speak. Now that my speech was over, I could relax. I looked around a bit while listening to Allie Hixon and let her words sink in. She was passionate and defiant as she talked about women's achievements in Kentucky.

I did not realize she was reading a prepared speech until I glanced her way. She seemed so spontaneous, so conversational, and so passionate. When she looked up at the crowd, she seemed to be talking directly to me and to the person beside me and to a person over by the stage. She made me proud of our accomplishments, proud of the fight. She rallied the crowd. Someday, I want to be able to do that.

Once Allie Hixon finished speaking, the formal part of the celebration was over. Everyone began milling about, visiting booths. An older woman with white hair walked toward me, smiling shyly. She was wearing a tidy dark skirt, a long-sleeved blouse, and a sweater over her shoulders. "Hello," she said as she approached me, "my name is Martha Asher and I—"

"I know who you are. I remember you," I responded. Instantly it was 1954 when I became sick from polio at Girl Scout camp. Martha was the camp nurse. "I've always wondered how you were," she continued. "Then I saw your name on the list of speakers for today. How are you?"

"I'm fine. I'm doing great! I'm happy, I really am. I have a master's degree. I've been a teacher. Now I'm doing disability advocacy. I think this is what I'm supposed to be doing." I had a deep sense that she needed to hear that my life was all right, that I had turned out okay. She seemed relieved.

We exchanged phone numbers, and I found out Martha was a born volunteer. She volunteered at Actors Theatre of Louisville. She searched junk stores, antique stores, people's homes, looking for props for the plays. She was an ATL associate and helped find housing and provide meals for the apprentice actors. Once we got to know each other better, she volunteered at *The Disability Rag*'s office (at Mary's house with four cats). I learned from Mary that Martha had always been dismayed that she had not recognized my symptoms sooner.

Martha became a mom figure for me, the mom I might have had if my mother had gone back to teaching after we were born. Martha was the kind of mom who would tell me that what I was doing was important and she would be supportive however she could. She sometimes provided me with a meal by taking me out to dinner (I would always try to get a doggie bag for Michael). And sometimes she created opportunities for me, like the time she donated money to my organization so I could hire a part-time office assistant for three months. Whenever I had office assistance I was more productive.

Martha also introduced me to good resources like the Jefferson County chapter of the National Organization for Women, where I experienced sisterhood for the first time. There are all kinds of people there, women and men, diverse people who all bring something to the organization, help each other, and respect each other's missions, even though they do not always agree or understand. They have a sense that what happens to one happens to us all.

I am so glad Rebecca got me that speaking gig.

Around this time, I found out that being known as an activist can be a drawback: People come to expect it of you. One night my friend Jerry and I went to a performance of *The Elephant Man* at the Macauley Theater on Broadway, downtown. Tim, one of our VISTA volunteers, went with us. I called ahead to order the tickets and to explain that I used a wheelchair. The theater's policy allowed only one "companion" to sit in the back "with the wheelchair." I told the box office I was coming with two friends and wanted to sit with them, not in the rear wheelchair section.

I paid for a seat in the same row as Jerry and Tim, but I sat in the aisle. Soon an usher approached us. "Excuse me, but the wheelchair has to move." This man spoke as politely as anyone would want, but he never looked directly at me. He talked over my head to my friends.

But I talked back to him. "I've paid for a seat in this row," I pointed out.

"You're a fire hazard," he insisted. "We have special handicapped seating, you know. We have a nice place for wheelchairs in the back row."

Tim had a flair for the dramatic and he liked using it. He pulled himself up to his full height and pointed: "You mean all the way back *there?*"

"Yes, back there," said the usher, matching Tim tone for tone.

Timmy took him on: "While you're at it, do you have a back seat from a bus we could sit on? Or maybe a lunch counter we can't use?"

The remark seemed lost on the usher. "It's the back row or else," he said. Or else what? I said I would not move; if they wanted me moved, they would have to move me themselves—which is exactly what I was beginning to think they might do. The usher walked away.

Now I know better what Angela must have felt that afternoon we went to a movies in 1959. She was the daughter of a friend of Chris's, my age, fourteen, and even though she was paid to spend the afternoons with me, we became friends and she taught me a lot. She lived in the real world; I did not. She told me I did not have to pretend that my mom had "spells." She knew my mother drank.

Every other Saturday, Angela took me out. Sometimes we went downtown. Angela, my manual wheelchair, and I would all fit in the back seat of a cab. One day we decided we take in a movie at the Mary Anderson Theater. Angela pushed my wheelchair up next to the ticket window and went up to the window herself. She asked the man what time the movie started. He told her and she told me. Then she asked him how much it cost; he told her and she told me. We figured out that we had enough money, so Angela put the money up in the window and said, "We'd like two tickets, please."

"Sorry, I can't let you in."

I asked the man, "Can't I sit in the aisle in my wheelchair?" I knew that when I had gone to the movies with my family, my father had lifted me out of the wheelchair and put me in a seat. It was a fire hazard to have a wheelchair in the aisle, but when you are little they often let you.

But now the man said, "Not you, her," and pointed to Angela.

Angela just stood there, and I just sat there. Finally, we went away. It was the first time, I think, I had ever felt embarrassment for someone else. It was so humiliating. She had asked, "What time is the movie?" and "How much is it?" and he had not said anything until she gave him the money.

I was indignant. Angela was not. She was used to it, expected it. I could not understand why she couldn't be let in. She could walk. I totally accepted why I might not be allowed to go in, but I could not fathom that she could not.

"I'm gonna tell my daddy about this!" I told her. I was sure he would call the management and straighten things out. We would write to the papers. We would create a big stir. We would embarrass them. That was my first personal experience with racial segregation. I had not known what that kind of segregation meant. I did not know that it would take a great deal more than my daddy writing a letter to get things to change for Angela.

Even though I was a child, I was already in the grip of the gimp mystique. I had assumed it was perfectly all right for the theater to keep me out. It was separate but equal that kept Angela out. For us with disabilities today, it is "special."

Such a nice word—"special." How can you criticize somebody when they are doing something special for you? My friend Carole Esterle investigated her daughter's special education classes in the mid-1980s and discovered them to be little more than a baby-sitting service. The school attitude had been: They cannot join the other kids, so have them go into this room and read, play, or whatever. When Carole decided her daughter should be mainstreamed, she had to hire a tutor to get her to the level of her classmates because she had spent too much time in "special ed." As my friend Janet says, "Special education is neither special nor is it an education." Too often, "special" is segregation; segregation is discrimination. It took a long time for some of us to recognize that we faced segregation, just like Angela did.

And we accept the lack of access and accommodation, just as Angela accepted segregation. It is hard to rebel against what society has taught us is our place. When nondisabled people think about a disabled person they know, they simply think, "That's Cass," or "That's Ron," or "That's Myrna." They do not think of us as part of a civil rights movement—or even as in need of one. Somehow, we can see how it was wrong for women and for black people to live with prejudice and exclusion. But society has such a negative impression of people with disabilities, it is hard to see that we are being excluded.

It is also hard for *us* to see that we are a part of a civil rights movement. For so long we have viewed our problems as medical or personal, rather than as the societal effects of exclusion and discrimination. We were taught to believe that each disabled person's situation was unique, "special"—any problems we faced were due to our own specific disability, rather than to group treatment like denial of accommodation. Everybody had been taught this, disabled and nondisabled people alike. This was one of the most handicapping aspects of the gimp mystique.

Many disabled people feel secure with "special," because it is all we have ever known. We accept our "special" services, just as Angela accepted segregation. It is hard to unlearn what society has taught us.

When the Macauley Theater usher and the box office manager came over to me in the aisle, I felt sick. It's easier to denounce an injustice toward someone else than to let yourself feel it when it happens to you. Being humiliated is bad enough—but to rise up and draw attention to it! I was not being a good girl and going to the back row. I should know better than to try to sit somewhere we don't belong. How awful of us to create a problem for the ushers!

They again told me I was a fire hazard. I politely explained that when I ordered my ticket, I said I used a wheelchair and that I wanted to sit with my friends. "They sold me this ticket, and I'm staying here," I said.

"When the fire marshal comes, he will insist you move," the manager continued. Everyone around us could hear this conversation.

I sounded firm but I felt hot; my underarms were damp. "I'll wait for the fire marshal then," I told him. To this day I do not know why I said it. It really was not like me at all. I think I had simply, finally, become angry that I could not even go out with friends, sit with them, and enjoy a play.

By now, Tim and I were getting looks of irritation from the people around us. All they could see was that the wheelchair woman was creating some sort of a problem for the usher. How thoughtless!

We were being unpleasant. Community organizing taught me that most people do not like public unpleasantness. I was hoping, as community organizing also taught, that the theater management would not want to call more attention to the situation. Apparently they did not see the irony of a crippled person being segregated from her friends at *The Elephant Man*, a play about a disabled man trying to live like everyone else. I am glad I had already read the play, because I do not recall seeing much of it that night. I had a hard time enjoying the evening. I kept looking over my shoulder for the fire marshal. He never showed up.

Not long afterward, the Macauley Theater became the focus of activism for some of us who use wheelchairs. One of Louisville's oldest theaters, it was the venue for classic concerts, the opera, and musicals. We felt we should be able to enjoy this theater and other events in Louisville as the rest of the community did, which included being able to sit in more than one location at the Macauley.

Much of my advocacy work has been with arts groups. Right after the 504 regulations were signed and the National Endowment for the Arts completed drafting its own regulations, I received a phone call from a very nice-sounding man, Irwin Picket, at the Kentucky Arts Council. He told me he had been appointed the staff person in charge of 504 compliance for our state arts council. He was calling Prime Movers, Inc., because he needed help.

He, I thought, had come to the right organization; still, I was surprised he called us. I was not used to others asking disabled people about disability issues. More often, nondisabled people thought we could not possibly know either what was best for us or how to find solutions to problems that affected us.

There was something else unusual about Irwin Picket: He seemed excited about working to assure that disabled people could participate fully in the arts experience. And he made me excited. "Just think," he exclaimed, "there's a whole new audience out there, people who have never experienced the opera or plays. This is going to be a challenge!" Here was a man who understood what we'd been preaching for years, and he had not even heard our sermon.

"You know," he continued, "before this 504 stuff, I never even thought, hmm, there are no disabled people here. Why not?" For the first time in my disability advocacy experience, I was talking to someone who really believed that we deserved the right to art. Yes, the law demanded it, but beyond the law, we deserved it.

Irwin's enthusiasm became what I have since called "the spirit." He had the spirit. He saw a mission: Art is a wonderful gift and he was going to be a part of giving that gift to disabled people.

But such good deeds take time. Several years after that phone call, a group of us organized the Task Force on Accessible Theaters because we were frustrated at the lack of enough accessible wheelchair seating in local theaters. With the help of the Kentucky Arts Council (KAC), we called for a meeting at the Macauley Theater between disability people and the Louisville arts groups that used the theater for their performances. The KAC was instrumental in funding various arts groups and could withhold funds from groups that were not accessible, so they encouraged people to come to the meeting. The Council wanted us to have the big stick. I think they were counting on us, the disabled folks, to hold these groups accountable.

At the meeting, Carole Esterle sat on the stage and I sat in front. Carole was an activist mom who had been involved in civil rights activities in college. She was interested in making sure her daughter lived as full a life as she wanted. Carole did not want her daughter segregated from the family in the back row for the *Nutcracker*. She brought an energy and anger to our group. When she was around I felt stronger.

Representatives from six local arts groups (including some board members), the state arts council, and even the public relations director of the Louisville Zoo came to the meeting, along with other members of our task force and a couple of reporters.

We were asking for simple equality. People using wheelchairs should have a right to the best seats in the house, as well as the midrange seats and the cheap seats. They should be able to sit with friends. It was not a complicated notion. Alberta Allen, a longtime board member of the Louisville Orchestra and a well-known fund-raiser for the arts, stood and asked, "Cass, what, specifically, should we do?"

We suggested they remove two seats in each of various areas of the theater. Mrs. Allen looked toward the manager of the Macauley. "Can we do that?" He mumbled something and finally said yes. She said, "Then we'll do it."

A year after that meeting, the Macauley insisted it had changed its ways and there would be no problem if someone in a wheelchair wanted to attend a performance. A few of us planned a theater outing to see if this were true, including Carole Esterle, Mary Johnson, and me. Carole had a van equipped with a wheelchair lift, so she offered to pick me up. Mary was nondisabled, but, for this occasion, she would pretend to be a wheelchair user. Mary had been on the front line for local issues and very often had the energy and muscle (physical and psychological) to get things done. She still got frustrated at the lack of outrage expressed by our local disability community over the absence of access and accommodation. "I just don't see why gimps don't speak up more," she would say to me. "If I were disabled . . ."

I had tried to explain the legacy of burdensomeness. Disabled people too often have to depend on the kindness of others, usually family members. If we ask for or expect very much, we are burdensome. Disabled people accept this oppression. "Try to see how you feel about activism once you're disabled," I had dared her. "See if you have any new thoughts." Accepting my dare, she would check out the Macauley by playing disabled for the evening.

Carole, Mary, and I wanted to see if the Macauley had removed seating in two new locations around the theater. The three of us had discussed strategy earlier in the day. I bought tickets for Carole and me in one location. Carole bought a ticket for Mary in a section of the theater where they claimed to have removed seating to open up space for wheelchairs. It had not been removed two days earlier when we checked, and we suspected it had not been removed even now, the night of the performance.

Before we got out of the van at the Macauley parking lot, Mary sat herself in the manual wheelchair she had borrowed from me. She said she did not want passersby to see that she was not really a handicapped person—she might seem like a crackpot. As Mary began to wheel herself out onto the van lift, it tottered three feet above the sidewalk. "Somebody hold me!" she hollered.

"You nervous?" I asked. I could not help myself. How many times had she mocked my nerves on this very lift? How often had she railed that disabled people were too timid to try the lifts on city buses?

Mary had been in a wheelchair before. Our VISTAs had considered them "disability cool" and sat around in the office in ratty, yard-sale wheelchairs. They casually offered them to bureaucrats at meetings, having made sure that an empty wheelchair or two were the only seats available. They found the experience good for shaking up consciousness.

Mary waited patiently while Carole got me out of the van and closed it up. She automatically began pushing Mary along the sidewalk. I was a little surprised Mary did not push herself along; she was pretty macho in her nondisabled life. It must be because the sidewalk slanted toward the street; it is hard to push a wheelchair if you are not used to it. She told me later she did not push herself because she did not want her hands or coat sleeves dirty from rubbing against the wheels, and Carole was right there, offering to push her, offering to take over for her. Mary exchanged her image of independence for clean clothes and hands.

At the theater entrance, a smiling couple held both doors wide open for us. I think because there were two wheelchairs, we looked like a parade. I waited for Mary's usual bluster about how society thought nothing of installing automatic doors for grocery carts but could not be bothered to install them for people. But Mary was changing before my eyes.

Pre-wheelchair, Mary never stopped moving. She devised elaborate projects and carried them out—with or without help. She weeded her garden, schemed over an advocacy project, got a few thousand brochures printed, and painted the kitchen—all at the same time. Getting dirty never bothered her. Now, all of a sudden, she was meek and tidy. She told me later she would have said something about automatic doors had she been standing up. But from her wheelchair, it just seemed too much bother. The timing was wrong. It was a lovely evening out with friends enjoying a concert. She did not want to spoil it by calling attention to herself. "After all," she said, "they were helping Carole with the heavy doors."

We were shown to our seats. As we had suspected, Mary's orchestra-section P13 seat was still quite firmly attached to the floor; it had not been removed as promised.

What we had not anticipated was Mary's response. "Let's just stay here," she pleaded. "Let's not go back and argue. I'll sit here in the aisle and maybe they won't notice." But we were on a mission; we returned to the box office. The ticket counter was too high for Mary to complain effectively; the box office manager would have to lean over the counter be able to hear her. Mary felt that Carole, standing, would be more forceful.

It took awhile to make the management understand that not one but two people in wheelchairs at the concert that night wanted to sit in the areas where the removable seats were. The management became apologetic. There must have been a terrible misunderstanding, the box office manager said to Carole. Their embarrassment was genuine, Mary decided. No one ever meant to cause a problem. The manager apologized and asked Mary if she would mind taking a seat in another location—a better seat, actually, for the same price.

Mary capitulated. "I just wanted to get parked where I belonged and get all this over with," she told me later. Because she was using a wheelchair, Mary sat head and shoulders above the concert-goers around her. She worried that someone in the theater might recognize her and accuse her of impersonating a disabled person. But people ignored her completely. After the Mendelssohn piece, she told me, she became bored. She wanted to yawn but worried that people would notice. She could not even fidget without worrying that she was drawing attention to herself.

At concert's end, we wheelchair people stayed put until the theater had mostly cleared. Then I went down my aisle, across the front of the theater, and up Mary's aisle. "Do you need help getting up the aisle?" I asked, trying not to have too much fun at her expense.

"No!" she snapped, struggling to turn her wheelchair around on the incline. She accepted gratefully when an usher offered to help her up the steep aisle into the lobby. There she wheeled about, acting like a regular disabled person. And like a regular disabled person, Mary had been grateful for a better seat. She accepted the management's apology for a "genuine mix-up"; she did not make a scene.

What about the issue of speaking out? When I prodded Mary she said she felt curiously unconcerned. "The concert was over.

I just thought, well, it all worked out okay really." Mary had succumbed to the gimp mystique. She had joined "the true silent majority," as Itzhak Perlman calls us. "The minute you sit in a wheelchair, attitudes are different. It's that basic."[2]

Mary now understood why disabled people did not complain more. She began to be impressed at the few of us who continued to work for the movement in spite of the obstacles our own minds set up. She was beginning to see why most disabled people were more concerned about attitudes than access, even when the lack of access kept them physically trapped.

"I don't want to be crippled anymore," Jewell told me. She was the first disabled woman with whom I felt a sisterhood. Our work in disability rights at the Center for Accessible Living was for each other. We had been sisters since that day she called me in the country offering to be my friend. She had helped with my finances and bookkeeping; I had helped with her grammar and spelling. We trusted each other deeply.

Jewell used the word "crippled" easily. For years I battled to overcome my aversion to the word—especially since FDR used it about himself. "Crippled," Jewell said, was how you felt when society put up so many barriers that you could not live a "normal" life, much less a successful one. Society treats people with disabilities like cripples, she said.

Jewell and I did not like each other when we first met. She had grown up in the city, I in the country. She lived with her large family in a small house; we had a large house. I had a master's degree; she graduated high school. I was prim and proper; she was tough and true. And I think we resisted because others kept trying to get us together.

The first time I saw Jewell was at a legislative committee meeting in our state capital in the late 1970s, where we were all lob-

---

2. Mary Johnson, "An Interview with Itzhak Perlman," *The Disability Rag*, February 1983, 8.

bying to add access requirements to the building code. Jewell and I did not formally meet that day, but we did size each other up. I sat in the back of the room and watched to see if she was as wonderful as everyone claimed.

They were right about her hair, thick, long, and red. Her waist was small, her chest ample. She wore a bright pink blouse and stiletto heels, used a motorized wheelchair, never walked, seldom stood. But she wore high heels. (I wore ballet shoes because they were easy.) The heels made her legs look great. She sat leaning forward in her chair, looking ready to bolt from the room if something displeased her. She sat with her leg up, ankle across her knee, like guys do. (She told me later that crossing her leg that way helped her keep her balance.) Her makeup complemented her coloring and her bright eyes. Her nails were long, perfectly shaped, painted. I was jealous.

Throughout the meeting, she talked to the two friends she had come with—loudly. She criticized the speakers who said that changing the regulations would mean increased construction costs, that lowering the height of pay phones would cause problems. Her tone was skeptical, her comments rude (I heard the word "crock" more than once).

I did not like her. She was making a spectacle of herself. I was sure she was unaware how easily she could be heard. Soon I realized she did not care. Her comments were right on target—and the people around her knew it. Many came up afterward and thanked her and asked more questions. Jewell was not articulate, but she had a way with words. She also had charisma. She did not know she had it; she did not know the word. But I saw it that first day. It was her red hair that attracted people, some said. "She's so self-assured, she struts," someone else added. But it was more: Jewell had presence. She came into a room and heads turned. Her firmness and determination made her appear strong.

Even after we became close friends, we had some falling-out periods. (When we got involved with the same man, I had to refine my definition of "sisterhood.") But we seemed to always know we would be honest with each other when we had to be. We always gave each other what we needed at the time.

My friend, my sister, Jewell Bourland died in April 1999 in her early fifties. I was not ready.

"Cassie, I don't want to be crippled anymore," she would say when she was tired of the fight. The last time she said those words to me, she had just gotten back from the state capital, from our semi-annual ritual of trying to get legislators to understand how liberating personal assistance is, how inexpensive it is, and, how absurd and expensive it is to confine anyone to nursing homes. Jewell was tough, but she was worn out.

I had called her to tell her some good news: A publisher was interested in my book. Without a pause she said, "Are you going to tell them how hard it is being a cripple?"

"Yes, Jewell."

"Are you going to tell them it doesn't have to be this way? That it's because of their stupid prejudice and their stupid belief that we don't matter? That that's what makes it so much harder than it has to be?"

"Yes," I answered. "I'm going to try."

"Good," she said.

5 True Hero

At the top of the villa stood a sloping tower six stories high with a magnificent view of the snow-capped mountains. It was the view Churchill wanted to share with the president . . . . The steep, winding stairs were too narrow to accommodate Roosevelt's wheelchair, so Mike Reilly and George Fox made a cradle with their hands to carry him step by step to the top, his legs . . . dangling like the limbs of a ventriloquist's dummy.
—Doris Kearns Goodwin, *No Ordinary Time*

FRANKLIN ROOSEVELT hid his disability from the public simply because he knew what public perception could do to his image. He did not hide it from Winston Churchill because he did not fear Churchill's perceptions. Churchill knew he was capable, a leader and a peer. And to people who were close to him, he was grand just the way he was.

Doris Kearns Goodwin wrote in *No Ordinary Time* (page 408): "At the topmost terrace . . . the president sat with Churchill for half an hour, gazing at the purple hills, where the light was changing every minute. 'It's the most lovely spot in the whole world,' the prime minister remarked. . . . [Later,] as the president's plane took off, Churchill put his hand on American Vice-Consul Kenneth Pendar's arm. 'If anything happened to that man,' he said, 'I couldn't stand it. He is the truest friend; he has the farthest vision; he is the greatest man I have ever known.' "

Roosevelt as hero is a contradiction, because people think he passed as nondisabled. His experience suggests that you can

---

The epigraph is from Doris Kearns Goodwin, *No Ordinary Time: Franklin and Eleanor Roosevelt—The Home Front in World War II* (New York: Simon and Shuster, 1994), 408.

achieve great heights as a disabled person only if you have re-sources that let you convince others you are not really that dis-abled. Many disabled people are angry at FDR because he hid his disability.

For me Roosevelt proved you can be seriously disabled and still do what you need to do. He had a real life, not that of an invalid. He did what he wanted. He could not be cured but he could have a normal life. And that is all I ever wanted. I never wanted to be president but—with resources—I could be whatever I wanted to be.

When I moved back to Kenwood Hill in the mid-1980s, it was my first opportunity to live a normal life. Living in Prospect and in Lyndon was hard, because we did not have much money. In Prospect, we had to watch the fuel gauge in the winter; we could barely pay for the propane so we waited to the last minute to order more. In Lyndon, my bedroom was right over the furnace. I also had an electric blanket, so I never had to turn the heat vents on in my room. We invested in a cast-iron wood-burning stove for the living room (Michael's room) and saved a lot by burning wood and by not living much beyond the living room or my bedroom in the winter. I did not know until years later that Daddy was afraid for me. He thought I was going to die in a fire or freeze to death. Yes, we roughed it, but I felt like I was living a pioneering life and I was pretty successful at it.

So I was ambivalent when our landlord died, his children sold the house we rented to developers, and we had less than two months to find a new place to live. When Daddy suggested our family's Kenwood home, as much as I loved the country, I was ecstatic at the prospect.

Mom was not. My move prodded Mom—bulldozed her, some people might say—out of the Kenwood house, where she lived alone. Shortly after I moved into my first apartment in the mid-Seventies, Mother and Daddy separated. A couple of years later, Mom decided this house was much too large for her.

Of course it was: three stories, four bedrooms, two and one-half bathrooms, and three-quarters of an acre of land. Daddy found retirement boring and unproductive, so he began buying rental property. Healthy and energetic, he felt he could do most of the maintenance himself and make more money. He started with apartments, but soon he had six buildings and three houses, if you counted Kenwood—and he did. Daddy saw Kenwood as just another piece of property he would sell as soon as Mom finally moved out.

He did not take good care of it when Mother lived there. When it needed painting, young guys, Michael's friends who worked for Dad, did the painting (for, I'm sure, barely minimum wage). They were fast but sloppy. Mother said that she could have done a better job if she were physically able. When the house was new, she had done much of the painting, especially the windows, and she was good at it.

After years of complaining about the house being too large for her, Mom saw my need as pushing her out of her house. Daddy, of course, saw this as a way to save money; he would not have to pay my rent at Kenwood. My life and my mother's needs were clashing again. Daddy pushed her to move; my deadline sealed her fate. She moved to an apartment, and I moved back home.

Michael made several trips in our Chevette that day, moving clothes and small items, while the movers took the big stuff. My wheelchair, my purse, my bookbag, and myself were part of the final load he moved from Lyndon to Kenwood. It was dark when I arrived there. Michael parked the Chevette in the garage and carried me up the same basement steps my dad used to carry me up. I was not apprehensive with Michael. I was not wearing braces with my feet sticking out; I gave them up when Chris began picking me up to put me in the car during my college years. I was smaller, less awkward to pick up, without braces. I never stood anymore, so what was the point?

Michael carried me around the first floor for a grand tour. Everything was in the correct room, but there were boxes everywhere, and after the tour, he carried me to Mom's bedroom—now mine—and put me in the bed. While not the biggest in the house, the room was large enough to hold my bed, a dresser, two chests of drawers, a bedside table, my own fainting couch, and my work-table.

I was not very comfortable in my wheelchair. Mary used to complain that they should make designer wheelchairs; all I ever wanted was one that fit me, something customized. Most wheel-chairs were built with the physique of a six-foot, straight-backed man in mind. I was five feet, four inches tall and had a crooked back and crooked legs. In the old days at Warm Springs, the brace shop was conscientious about adapting equipment to each person. Today that kind of attention is usually not provided when you get a new chair.

Now, because this house was so accessible to me, I began getting up in my chair more, and the first thing I did once I was settled at Kenwood was call the Center for Accessible Living for a ramp. When I lived here as a child, I had to go up the concrete ramp Daddy built from the driveway to the backyard, then travel a sidewalk that went around the back of the house to the patio, and up a small wooden ramp from the patio to the porch. On the screened porch, there was a step up to the living room. Since I did not have a motorized wheelchair in those days, I could not move around on my own. There was always someone to get me up that one step into the house.

I was proud of the Center's ramp-building program. It began with Prime Movers, Inc., and our VISTA volunteers. As we sat around talking one day, frustrated that more people did not attend the workshops PMI offered, we realized that people who did not have ramps could not get out of their house to come to the workshops. I had been lucky with ramps. Daddy built them at Kenwood and Cherokee Road. The houses we rented in the country were combinations of old country houses combined to make a larger house, and we never had a landlord refuse to let us build ramps. At Prospect, Michael built two. At Lyndon, he built one into the house and one from the living room to the dining room.

Since the majority of disabled people are poor, many we knew did not have an easy way to get a ramp or to pay for it. No one was really building ramps in those days. Mary and some of the VISTAs wondered, How hard could it be? What do we need to build them? How long will it take? They talked to carpenters about plans, they got donated wood and supplies, and they built ramps. Mary even wrote a booklet, a step-by-step plan to make a ramp.

The first ramps were built with VISTA volunteers and donations. Once the Center for Accessible Living started, the project developed into the Ramp Builders Program, with staff and grants and donations from various sources, including individuals, Community Development funds, and local politicians who realized if their constituents could not get out of house, they couldn't vote.

From the house in Kenwood, I called the Center and got my name on the list. I did not own the house, so Daddy had to give them permission to build. Considering he was getting something for free, he did not hesitate to sign. In the months before they could get to me, I relied on the trough ramps I later took to Claudette's to get in and out. Here at Kenwood, the ramps had to cover only four steps so they were not steep, but they were wobbly, so I never went up them by myself.

Finally the ramp builders from the Center came. First, they replaced the concrete ramp from the driveway to the backyard and added a handrail. ("Concrete" probably is not accurate. Daddy had built the ramp inexpensively by using an experimental coating for the concrete. It turned out to be slippery so he mixed the second batch with gravel. Now we had a mess of broken, gravely, unsafe concrete.) Next the builders put in a ramp with handrails that followed along the side of the house, not taking up room on the patio. Daddy original wooden ramp from the middle of the patio to the screened porch had made the patio practically unusable.

Kenwood, I soon realized, was the most accessible place I had ever lived. I had a motorized wheelchair, so I could get into all the rooms on the first floor. I could go in the basement, if I wanted to, although I had to go outside and around the back of the house to the driveway and the basement door.

When I was a little girl, I sort of thought this house was built for me. It had always been pretty accessible, especially with ramps. All the rooms on the first floor are big, the hallway wide. But the more I got around the house and neighborhood with a motorized wheelchair, the more amazed I was that I had managed this before I became so "able." Looking back, I experienced a great deal of life for a "crippled person." And, at the same time, I was thunderstruck by how much more I could have accomplished with a motor.

I did not have a motorized chair until I was thirty-two, when Vocational Rehab bought one for me. They thought it would make me more employable.

Sometimes it is not a question of money or vans—or employment. One day, I was waiting with a new friend in the hall after a Human Relations Commission committee meeting. We both used wheelchairs so we could "stand around anywhere" as long as we were out of the way. Jack was not a committee member but was taking a class at University of Louisville that required him attend court hearings. Since the courtroom was minimally accessible, he came to the Handicapped Citizens Committee to report his experience. He seemed young and shy, but he was strong when he talked about trying to be a part of something that was inaccessible to him. I was impressed and hoped he would get involved with the committee.

Jack did not have motors on his chair. He could push himself around some, very slowly, very labored. I noticed he did not do it if there was someone nearby to push him. I asked him why he did not have a motorized wheelchair and he said: "I don't really need one. I get around okay and it's good exercise for me." (I do not know any fitness expert anywhere who advocates wheelchair pushing for fitness!)

"Besides, I am seldom by myself," he continued. "I'm usually with my mom, dad, or sisters." Jack looked at his watch and excused himself. "I want to use the restroom. If my mom comes . . ." I nodded him on.

The restroom was way down the hall. He had barely reached the door when a woman walked up to me and asked, "Do you know where the Handicapped Citizen's Committee meets?"

"Are you Jack's mother?" I introduced myself and explained where her son was. She and I got into a conversation, and the subject of Jack and a motorized wheelchair came up. His mother responded right away: "Oh, Jack doesn't need a motorized wheelchair to get around. He never goes anywhere by himself. He always has one of us with him."

One thing independent living teaches you is that each of us has the right to determine how we want to live. Some of us want to be as independent as possible, to have our own apartments, to have jobs if we can, and live on our own. Some of us are most comfortable living in the security of a family. So I could not say that Jack's going nowhere on his own unless he scheduled around his very active family was not the best living arrangement for him.

He was like Jewell. When Jewell became the president of the board of directors for the Center for Accessible Living one year after it opened, she was living with her family. Some people criticized her because they thought she should live on her own. Jewell explained that at her house she was never without help, and her family was large and dependable. It was not the kind of independence I wanted, but it worked for Jewell. She did most of what she wanted in life and she did a lot of it without leaving her bedroom. She was the best president of the board for over fifteen years.

In the accessible environment of my home in Kenwood, I went into each of the rooms on the first floor to see how it felt to sit there. The house has windows everywhere. I started by sitting close to the big bay window in the dining room. In the winter, when the trees were bare of leaves, I could see the lights of

Iroquois Manor Shopping Center about three-fourths of a mile away.

I also sat the living room in the corner once occupied by Mom's gold-striped upholstered armchair, where I had often sat during parties we had when Mom and Daddy were at Lake Cumberland. From those windows, I could see the hill change—the dogwoods and redbuds bloom in the spring; the burning bushes and trees turning orange, yellow, and red in the fall.

Because the house was so accessible to me, I ran around a lot outdoors, too. Once the ramps were built and the living room door was left open, I started running in and out a lot. For the first time, I realized I lived on a hill. When I lived with Mom and Dad, even though I had a pretty active life, I was usually in bed when I was home. Since I did not have a motorized wheelchair, when I was up in my chair, I did not move around the house much. I was not in the yard unless I was coming and going to the car. I never really came in and out enough to realize I lived on such a hill.

I loved knowing that Cherokee Indians watched buffalo herds follow a trace to the Falls of Ohio from the tops of Kenwood and Iroquois Hills. In the old days there was a small sawmill on Kenwood Hill and a rock quarry. Otherwise the hill remained practically untouched, with a few homes and elaborate log cabins serving primarily as summer homes where the wealthy could escape the heat of the city. The community was christened Kenwood Hill in 1890 when the Kenwood Park Residential Company bought the land and developed it. It remained sparsely populated until the 1940s. Mom and Daddy bought their land in 1941 and moved into the house they built in 1942. By 1948, the hill had been carved up by developers and, by the 1960s, most of the hill was developed.

The developers failed to take drainage into account. Cutting down all the trees created severe water runoff problems and extensive soil erosion, damaging the forest, roads, and house foundations—including ours. Not one year passed without the basement flooding. Water seeped in through the unfinished "dirt" room, or the basement bathroom window, and trickled—or streamed—across the basement floor to the garage door and out into the drain in the driveway. The basement had only a laundry area and Daddy's workbench and was mainly used as a garage, so the water was a bother but not a disaster. I used to think if we were rich, Daddy would have made that dirt room into recreation room.

When I moved back to Kenwood, Michael fixed the basement up as a studio where he could listen to and produce music; when he had a band, they practiced down there. Water trickling through musical equipment was *not* acceptable. Whenever we heard a bad weather forecast, Michael began a "here comes the rain" ritual that included making sure everything was out of the path of the water; once the heavy rains came, he frequently checked the hose that siphoned water out of the dirt room and into the basement drain to prevent a real flood. Often he had to suck on the hose to get the siphoning process started. We lived through one rainy season before Michael fashioned a trough outside the dirt room to carry the first overflow to the basement drain. He did not like the siphoning part.

I also loved living in a place with a history. A log cabin on the Hill's Possum Path was once the home of two Louisville teachers, Mary and Patty Hill. Patty was credited with writing the lyrics to "Happy Birthday." Three cabins on Kenwood Hill Road owned by Lou Tate became known as the Little Loomhouse. Two of them housed looms where all the kids in the neighborhood took weaving classes, including my sister, my brother, and me (before I had polio). The Little Loomhouse cabins are on the National Register of Historic Places.

The rugged hill makes a great environment for birds, including owls and hawks, and squirrels, rabbits, chipmunks, snakes, possums, raccoons and—some people have claimed—foxes. Mother says she killed copperheads in our backyard when we were little. Kenwood Hill in the spring feels and sounds like an aviary, and the blooming dogwoods, redbuds, orange blossoms, forsythia, and creeping myrtle and honeysuckle make our hill a sparkling, fragrant oasis in the city.

Now that I was back at Kenwood, with motors, I could see all this up close. I began to do ordinary things on my own, what most people call "running errands." Almost every Friday, after the mail came, I headed out of the house, through the backyard, down the driveway, across the street, down the sidewalk to the side street, and down that street for a block to Esplanade. At that point, I had to decide whether to go left or straight ahead. Turning left would take me to Third Street, a rather busy thoroughfare. Going straight would take me to the neighborhoods, places I walked to when I was little.

I usually headed down Tecumseh, left on Seneca Trail, and through side streets. I passed the big white house Mary's mom grew up in. Across the street was a small brick house with a tiny fenced-in yard. A little yappy dog lived there; when she was in the backyard, she barked at me. If I talked to her, she barked more. If I went close to the fence, she stopped barking and wagged her tail vigorously. I loved that dog.

Next, I crossed the street and passed the Catholic church where my brother was married and the elementary school next door. I tried to make this trek before school let out, because cars and buses are hard to maneuver around. I'm short and not easy to see.

The banks stayed open late on Friday, so I did not have to rush. I deposited most of my check and kept a little cash. Then I went to Hardees for a chicken sandwich. I always left a tip on my food tray because I could not reach the trash bin to dispose of my garbage. Then I was off to the shopping center. Iroquois Manor is an old strip mall with three sets of buildings, including a Walgreen's Drug Store, the Iroquois Bakery, a five and dime that turned into a dollar store, two women's clothing stores, a video store, the Peppermint Lounge, a Valumarket, a large Asian grocery store, a bridal shop, and a Porter Paint store. I went into lots of the stores, depending on the availability of people to be door openers. (Walgreen's and Valumarket were the only stores with automatic doors.)

Most often I frequented the Walgreen's and the bakery, which offered fresh unsliced bread, rye rolls, cookies for every occasion, and chocolate-covered apple fritters. Sometimes I stopped at one of the clothing stores, especially if it was having a sale; sometimes at the Valumarket for groceries; sometimes, depending on what we were doing to the house, at the Porter Paint store.

The thirteen blocks, or three-fourths of a mile, from Iroquois Manor to my house was all uphill. I was so happy to have motors! And I had a great time running errands.

I also liked riding buses—eventually. A couple of years after I moved back to Kenwood, and after years of fighting with the Transit Authority of River City (TARC) to get them to adhere to the law and put wheelchair lifts on buses, they began to do so— but slowly, and only on new buses. Only two routes would be accessible at first, the busiest, Fourth Street and Broadway. My routes! I could get almost anywhere in town on those two routes.

I no longer had to call two weeks ahead to schedule a ride with TARC3, the paratransit service, to converse with the schedulers.

"It would be easier to coordinate rides and serve you all better if you did not live all over town."

"You mean, we should all live in the same building, maybe?"

"Yes! Maybe not in the same building, but . . ."

"The same neighborhood?"

But also no more being picked up by a little bus or van at the end of my driveway. No more riding all over town with Mr. Rhodes. I was going to miss him and all he taught me about economy and dignity.

Now, on my own, I could go down my driveway, go three blocks from my house to Third and Esplanade, and catch a bus. Still, I felt apprehensive—scared, actually.

I consider myself macho. I had been stuck downtown with dying wheelchair batteries, and I had to get a stranger to call PMI so someone on staff could come rescue me. I recovered brilliantly when my battery case fell off of my chair, unplugging itself and stopping me in my tracks near Fourth and Broadway. I had to ask a stranger to reattach and replug my battery case—not an easy job since it is located under my chair and neither of us had a wrench. I told the young man who helped me I would give him money but I had none on me. He said that was okay and held up a small wrinkled brown-paper bag that obviously held a bottle.

"My reward is right here," he said. "You stop by that car dealer in the next block and make them tighten the screws to that battery case or it's going to come off again."

When I examined my fear about taking buses, I realized the source of my apprehension. I was getting a little tired of often being in the vanguard, the one to try something new first. But the Chevette died, and since Michael and I could not afford another car, it was the bus or nothing.

It took me a while to be comfortable catching buses, and it took a while to get the kinks out of the system. In the early days drivers did not know how to work the lift properly, although they had been trained how to use the equipment. And they knew the rules: wheelchair user gets on lift, in bus, and in the clamp tie-down unassisted; drivers assist with seat belt if needed. But we all needed experience—which I could not get if I didn't ride the buses.

"I'll get faster with more practice," I told one driver when it took me a while to get out of the bus tie-down and off the bus.

"Hope it ain't on my bus," he grumbled.

I ran home, called my friend Tina, the head of the paratransit department at TARC. "Tina, I think I just experienced a 'racial' slur and I'm not even black!" It *felt* like a slur.

Once I got over the early trials, I liked taking buses. Now I was able to ride through neighborhoods where I grew up. My bus to town took me past the apartment building Mom and Daddy lived in after they were married, while they saved their money for Kenwood. It took me past the branch library where my sister used to check out six books a week while I checked out only two (I was a slow reader). I rode past Churchill Downs and the old buildings that at one time had been Paw-Paw's taverns.

I had never been aware that my location had slowed me down. In the Kenwood house, the more I did, the more I wanted to do. One morning I left home around nine and took the bus downtown for a board workshop. After lunch, Sharon and I caught another bus to a shopping center for several hours of shopping and dinner. We expected to be tired out by evening, though, and had scheduled paratransit rides home. A normal day for most people, but for me a very busy day and a new experience.

If I was going to have a normal life, I decided, it was going to be here in Kenwood, and I was going to need more help. As I got more involved with the Center and our biannual fight with the Kentucky legislature, I met people like Claudette and Juanita, who helped me give Michael the time off he deserved to travel and to pursue his music. As Michael and I both began focusing on our "careers," we soon saw we were being pulled in different directions. We no longer needed each other in the same way. After ten years together, we did not have to be responsible for each other anymore. Not being dependent on each other was a good thing, we decided.

Michael helped me fly, but he was not interested in helping me have a career—nor should he have been. And I was tired of putting everyone else's needs before mine. Now we both had options.

I made appointments with two potential attendants to meet at pizza parlor near Iroquois Manor Shopping Center. One interviewee had a car; I scheduled her appointment at four o'clock (after her kids were home from school). The other, Juanita, rode the bus. I scheduled her for 1:30.

I had gotten Juanita's name from a list at the Center for Accessible Living, which had made efforts to find potential personal assistants by going to tech schools and talking up the program.

Unlike agencies, we do not have people running all over town to do a job; we offer flex hours and part-time work.

Juanita later told me that when she was in elementary school, a kid hit her in the head with a baseball bat, knocking her unconscious for a few seconds. When her family took her home, she fell asleep. When she woke up, she said, she could not remember things as well. Now that her own eighteen-year-old daughter had moved out, Juanita wanted to be independent of her father. When she found a brochure in her door about the nursing class at a nearby tech school, she took two hundred dollars she had saved from baby-sitting and went. She got herself back and forth on the bus, she took classes, and graduated with a nurse's aide certificate.

Juanita had a sweetheart reference, her teacher, who sounded on the phone like a great-aunt talking about her favorite niece.

I got to the pizza parlor at one o'clock, and Juanita arrived on time at 1:30. I had been watching the door, to have those few seconds to size her up before she spotted me. I make snap judgments about people, but I know it, and I am prepared to have my mind changed. When I saw Juanita come in the door, I knew she was my interviewee. I knew the minute I saw her that she was a respectful person, comfortable and good-hearted. She reminded me of myself, even with her extra thirty pounds and bleached blond, teased hair, too-dark thin eyebrows, and pink lipstick. She wore a big, puffy, hip-length pink coat. As I found out during our interview, we had a lot in common—our birthdays were three days apart; we both spent time in Fairdale, Kentucky (she lived there; I visited Maw-Maw and Paw-Paw on their farm there); and we both were being semi-kept by our fathers. We met each other at a good time.

Juanita really wanted work. She no longer got Social Security for a dependent child, and her dad had been paying her rent. She needed an income. She lived in the neighborhood and could get to my house easily. I told her I would call in a couple of days.

I waited until five o'clock, but my second interviewee never showed up. I called Juanita the next day and asked if she could come to my house for a second interview. That way she could see what she was getting into and meet Michael and my cats. She did not have a phone, so I relayed this through her father.

I knew right away I was going to hire her, but I wanted to start slowly. She began coming a couple of mornings a week, mainly to get me bathed, dressed, up in my chair. Sometimes she spent the night so I could get up and out early for meetings. And sometimes she stayed a couple of days so I could give Michael real time off.

Juanita did not do everything right. She did not do many things as well as Michael (she never could), but she was willing to keep trying and I tried to adapt whenever possible. I liked the girlie things she did with me, like fixing my hair or going shopping— just because we could. When I had people at the house for meetings, she made iced tea with fresh mint. I taught her to fix it the way Mom did. She was a good match for me, a few years older, and we enjoyed the same things. Two Tauruses, we understood each other.

Jewell, Sharon, and I had volunteered to take information-and-referral calls two to three days a week at the Center for Accessible Living to relieve staff. Many of the board members were people with severe disabilities. Some of us wanted to prove to staff that we could pull our own weight, that we were not just dictators, that we had a reason for being in a position of authority.

The three of us shared a desk at the end of a long row of cubicles in the big room, right in front of the closet door. People had to walk around us to get into the closet. Often they piled stuff on our desk, so the first thing we had to do when we got to work was rearrange the desk.

There was always a stack of phone calls to be returned. It bothered me when a long time had passed since a person had called. I had been a back-room person myself, and I knew how hard it was to call for help. You have to screw up your courage, you have find a convenient time to talk (with no family members around to interrupt), and you have to be able to deal with disappointment when answers or help is postponed. It is hard to take a step out of the routine you are in with your family. I wanted to be the kind of person I had needed when I called Mrs. Scott, the counselor at Family and Children's Agency. We did not have Mrs. Scott's credentials but, as volunteers, we were trained to know how to help people find a Mrs. Scott.

I was also concerned that, if calls were not returned promptly, the Center could get a bad reputation: "I called that Center, and they never called me back."

On one of my days in the office, the oldest call was from a person named Myrna Byerly. I was not sure how to pronounce her name. I was not good at pronouncing certain letter combinations, and I never learned what all those little symbols in the dictionary meant. I am especially bad with names. I do not appreciate it when someone calls me Irving, or Irwin, or Irvine. My name is Irvin. So I do not want to massacre someone else's name.

The Byerly part was okay. There is a big car dealership in Louisville called Byerly Ford. But the *Myrna* part. Let's see: My, Myron. Myron-a. Was that it? I kept wanting to say Myra, as in Myra Breckinridge. I looked at the pink slip of paper a long time. I called. Dialing out at the Center was difficult for me. You pushed a button to get a free line, then another to get an outside line. You had to make sure all the while that you did not inadvertently get on someone else's phone line. Pushing buttons in the first place is difficult for me.

The phone rang and rang. It may be part of the stereotype, but everyone knows that when you call a disabled person, you need to let the phone ring a long time. (I felt better when I read about phone etiquette in the phone book and it said the "courteous thing to do" is to let the phone ring fifteen times.) Finally someone answered. I said, "May I speak to Ms. Byerly?" I felt comfortable saying "Byerly." It was Myrna, who thanked me for letting the phone ring a long time. She said she had been down on her knees scrubbing the kitchen floor.

Her voice was soft. She talked slowly, deliberately. I needed to focus in on what she was saying to make sure I understood her. I asked her why, specifically, she had called the Center. She said she had seen our public service announcement on TV and she wanted to know more. PSAs are a burden to stations, since they do not get paid to air them, and they put them on late at night. The Center had a black-and-white cartoon with a wheelchair user going down a black-and-white street with unramped houses; a rainbow goes by, ramps appear at each house, and color abounds. *The Disability Rag* calls that "disability cool."

I asked questions to get Myrna talking more and learned that she had been going through a divorce. I asked about alimony; she said she was not asking for any. I said she needed a good lawyer; she said she did not want anything from her husband. She just wanted a new start.

I could tell she was sad. I told her a little history about the Center and the independent-living movement. I told her the Center was different because it was staffed and run by disabled people. I said I was disabled myself but I did most things and, with the help of programs at the Center, I could do lots more. She was shocked that I was a disabled person and surprised that I was a volunteer. I told her about the Center's counseling program, which might be helpful because she was going through a divorce. I told her about our housing program and Ramp Builders and how she could get a ramp. I told her about peer support and how someday she could give back by helping other disabled people take independent steps. I told her to call Annie King, our counseling program manager, and talk to her. And I told her she needed to come down and get to know us, because some of us were really cool. She said she would.

Months later I sat in our bimonthly peer support group waiting as people gathered. Of the Center's three peer support groups, one was made up of disabled people still living at home who needed peer support to become more independent; one was for newly disabled people who were dealing with big life changes;

and the third, our group, was made up of people living "on our own" (even if we were still living under our parents' roofs). Some of us had shared-living arrangements and were beginning to have new "families" of our own.

About eight of us had gathered, including Jewell, Sharon, Ken, and Robin, when Annie came into the room. She was not alone. "Is it okay if Myrna joins us?" It is important for the group to make such decisions, but we knew Anne would not introduce someone to the group who was not ready, so we welcomed the newcomer.

Annie suggested that we go around the room and introduce ourselves. We mentioned how long we had been coming to the Center, talked about being board members or on committees, or spoke of our disabilities. I always have to think a moment before I speak. I have been so involved for so long that I have a hard time deciding what to say. Do I say I was a part of the group that organized and got grants to get the Center started, that I had been involved with disability projects, or that I taught disability history and culture classes? This time I said, "I am Cass Irvin, I-R-V-I-N, and I have been involved with the Center as a client and volunteer for a while, and I like it." I also said something about writing for *The Disability Rag* and the Center's newsletter.

Two more people introduced themselves, then the newcomer: "My name is Myrna Byerly."

"Byerly?" I asked. "Like the Ford dealer?" Yes, Myrna answered. "Cool!" I responded. When you work in resource development you think of things like car raffles. Then I remembered her call, and I felt glad that she had come in.

She said, "You're Cass Irvin?" I nodded and she said, "You saved my life." She told us when she called the Center she was desperate. She could not get out of the house by herself; her children had grown up and left home, and that was hard because they had always helped her. She was going through a divorce that would leave her entirely by herself. "I just did not think there were any answers. And Cass called me from the Center when I was down on the floor scrubbing, with tears streaming down my cheeks. I was contemplating suicide. Cass told me to come down and meet the people here. You said they would be very nice and I would feel at home. You were right."

People always say, "If I could make a difference in one person's life, it's all been worth it." Myrna was my one person.

Myrna and I became close friends. Because she was just beginning to discover herself, she was like my little sister. But she is six years older than I, and she also became another mother, teaching me so much about perceptions and disability life. She had finished high school and gave up an opportunity to work for the FBI in Washington, D.C., to marry. She and her husband had two children and a chunk of the American Dream. She was a young wife and mother when she contracted encephalitis, an inflammation of the brain. Some people recover completely; some die. Myrna's vision was badly impaired, her speech slurred, her balance and coordination almost completely gone. But, slowly, she improved.

Her goal had been to "get well." "That was what I had to do. I had to get well. My family expected me to get well. None of us thought any different." Full figured, with an ash-blonde (from a bottle) bouffant hairdo, Myrna was my image of everybody's favorite Aunt Dorothy, the stereotypical 1960s housewife. "My kids, they were growing up, and I was supposed to be their mom, and I was supposed to 'do' for them. How could I do for them if I couldn't walk? So I had to get well, didn't I? Or at least try." For Myrna that meant going to therapy, doing what the doctor said.

"My husband had to do the shopping all the time. I couldn't get out of the house anymore."

To do laundry, "I'd get my 5-year-old to help," she said. "He'd carry that basket of dirty clothes down to the basement for me. I'd get down on my behind, then I'd bump down those steps after him. There were seventeen steps. I used to count them, because I had to bump myself back up again. I don't know why my husband never thought to bring the washer and dryer upstairs. I just learned how to manage."

Myrna's mother cooked and took over going to the children's school activities, PTA meetings, plays. Myrna could not get up the steps into the school. The reason she could not go to her children's school was because she was handicapped—that is how everyone saw it. It did not occur to anyone, including Myrna, that the problem was not so much her disability as that nothing was accessible to her.

For years, Myrna did not use a wheelchair; her family believed she should try to walk. Finally she got a scooter, but she kept it in a shed in the back yard. "We didn't have a ramp," she told me, matter-of-factly, "and my husband worried that the scooter would mess up the floors, so we didn't bring it in the house. I just did without."

My family had not really expected me to get better, and Myrna's life seemed foreign to me. According to psychologist Carol Gill, it was pretty typical. "We've been raised in families in the 'majority culture'—nondisabled—and have accepted that majority culture as our own. . . . We've been told, in many ways, that if we only worked hard enough to be 'normal'—meaning 'not disabled'—we'd be accepted as able-bodied. And we bought that thinking, and we worked hard. And yet we found that, no matter how hard we worked, we were not children by blood; we were only children by adoption."[1]

Once Myrna became involved with the Center, she realized that her disability was not the problem. A couple of years later, she told her story to a class at the Kent School of Social Work at the University of Louisville. I helped her prepare her remarks by recording what she wanted to say on my answering machine and then transcribing them. As a former English teacher, I edited them a bit, and I typed the final draft in large print so Myrna could read it easily. She told the class:

> My family, and society, very subtly taught me that I was not okay.
> They did this by not making any adjustments in my house to make

---

1. Gill is quoted in Johnson, "Emotion and Pride," 1.

it easier for me to do my laundry, cooking, cleaning, or caring for my two small children ages two and five.

From the beginning of my disability in 1966 until 1988, when I began weekly visits to the Center for Accessible Living, I had an extremely hard life. Just to get outside, my husband, or my dad, or one of my children (after they got big enough) would carry my wheelchair down the front steps and—holding tight to the banister—I could walk to my chair. Shopping was something horrible; rather than bother with taking me, I would make a list and my husband or Dad would pick up groceries, the kids' clothes, school items, and whatever else we needed. I could not get anywhere to take care of the activities of daily living and, for certain, nothing social. I would loved to have taken my kids swimming or to a park. Even their school was not accessible.

I could have handled my disability but it was the barriers I faced everyday that made my life so difficult.

Myrna's opinion of herself had been created by people who thought she should be nondisabled, achieve normalcy. That is the real "physical challenge," and it should not have to be that way. The only way Myrna could change the way she thought about herself was to get a job. I was concerned; we both knew she was not very "qualified." Her best qualification was typing, and she could no longer type. I knew she wanted to be a program director or a facilitator of peer-support groups, but she did not have the qualifications, the experience to direct programs, or the time to get that kind of education.

I was afraid Myrna would go to Vocational Rehab and the counselor would ask, "What do you want to do?" She would answer, "Be a social worker or counselor." And her VR counselor would probably recommend college or a two-year training program. But Myrna wanted a job, and I knew she did not want to wait.

Myrna was a disenfranchised housewife as much as a disabled person. Her husband was gone, her kids grown up and on their own. But because society was inaccessible to her, Myrna had not been president of the PTA or an organizer of church activities. Most women whose husbands left them after twenty-five years of marriage could create a decent resume from such experiences.

I suggested Myrna volunteer at the Center to get experience, develop a resume, and work her way up to a paid job. That is how the independent-living centers got started and how I got most of my experience: volunteering; taking on more and more; being responsible. It helped me develop the credentials I have for a real job.

We debated this issue often. Myrna knew she could not get well, as her family wanted, but she could work. She was of value. She was as good as anyone else. To Myrna, a job would prove to herself and her family that she was normal. The amount of money she made did not matter. Her paycheck was the proof.

A few weeks after she started a part-time job at the Center, Myrna called me, excited. "I got my first paycheck," she crowed. "It's not much—but I earned it!"

"I knew you could do it," I told her. She had not been so sure.

"I'm so slow—and because of my disability, I don't understand things right away. But they didn't pressure me."

"They accommodated you," I said.

"Yes," said Myrna, "they let me take my time. And I'm getting faster every day."

"Just like anyone learning a new job," I offered.

"That's right," Myrna said with recognition. "Just like anyone else." Myrna made my realize that I wanted a paycheck myself.

Perhaps because of my own physical circumstances, I never saw myself getting a "real" job—a nine-to-five, five-days-a-week job. I think people should be all they can be, but that does not have to include a job. I grew up thinking being a mother and housewife was fine. If you had the ability and opportunities to work, that was fine too. Myrna's view of a job as an indicator of value bothered me. If her view was correct, I did not have much worth.

Either as a volunteer or as a part-time employee, I had worked in the disability movement in Kentucky, trying to change society's view of persons with disabilities by speaking out and helping start disability organizations and programs. But while we all acknowledge how vital volunteers are, our society does think better of people who get paid—how else can society judge our worth or productivity? Disabled people accept this view, too: An associate of mine with a disability once told me he would value my opinion more if I were employed.

The reward for volunteering is spiritual. Spiritual is wonderful, but it does not pay the bills. And at this stage in my life, I found paying bills pretty important.

Myrna inspired me to want to work—Myrna and having responsibility for a house. We could not live like hippies anymore, I thought. Our Kenwood house had family history and traditions and style—and it needed attention. The walls needed painting; we needed venetian blinds to replace the curtains Mom took with her. Most of our furniture was hand-me-downs, like Mom's modern circular turquoise couch with stiletto legs, and needed replacing. We had a few nice things—Maw-Maw's oak pedestal table and Michael's mom's oak cane chairs—but we needed dishes and linens, all that regular stuff. And it all takes money.

Before I had moved out on my own with Willie, Daddy, my sister, and I came up with a budget that included money for a live-in attendant, food, rent, and utilities. Initially, Daddy paid all my expenses. Mom still gave me an allowance for spending money, the same amount I had in college. When I started teaching, Daddy cut back the amount he gave me proportionately. When he became eligible for Social Security, we found I could get benefits because I was considered a dependent. Since that again changed my income, Daddy cut back again. When I became a VISTA, he cut back more.

When my father began his real-estate "empire," he hired me as his agent at no salary (since he paid my expenses), which meant doing whatever he asked me to do: answer calls from ads, schedule appointments with the lady who showed apartments for Daddy and for Daddy to meet with new renters, check out rental applications, handle calls and complaints from tenants. I really could not object. When Daddy saved money, he could more easily afford to help me. But because he never gave me a cost of living raise, I found myself not telling him the truth about how much I made from workshops or consultations, just so Michael and I could have spending money.

As I sat in the cold in Lyndon one day, trying to pay bills and feeling poor, I figured out how much I got paid for working for Daddy. I was on call twenty-four hours a day—if someone locked themselves out of their apartment, they called me, day or night. But I was listed in the rental materials as available from 1:00 to 11:00 P.M., seven days a week—seventy hours a week. I figured I was making a little over a dollar an hour. It is a good thing I did not look at my "pay" as an indicator of my worth.

Now I had a subsistence income and a house I wanted to make into a home. How hard was I going to have to work to make enough money to pay for everything? People I knew who worked and lived on their own put in forty hours a week or more. I knew I could not do that. I was going to have to find something that could be adapted to my stamina.

Our Center was going through a period of board/staff clashes and we were looking for a new executive director. Jewell and I were frustrated because we could not find anyone with the right qualifications, experience, and perspective. We cared so deeply that we toyed with the idea of job sharing. I was great at grant writing, fund-raising, and program development and implementation. Jewell was great with budgets, accounts, staff policies, and so on. We had the right philosophy, and we knew what kind of job needed to be done to get the Center back on track.

When Jewell said she would job share with me, I knew we could do it, but I was scared. My resume looks good. Many people I know and respect had asked over the years, "Why don't you take the job?" Why did I doubt myself?

First, because of my credentials. I had done this kind of work before but in little pieces, like supervising staff at ALPHA. I never directed programming at the same time, nor had I been paid. My part-time jobs gave me a chance to rest up in between projects.

Despite twenty years of working in the disability movement in Kentucky, I had never "worked" full time, forty hours a week. During the twenty-five years I worked, I earned a salary for only five: two years as a teacher and three years as a VISTA. I had part-time jobs like directing projects or consultations where I prepared and conducted workshops or made presentations. I had a lot of opportunities to do grant reviews and panel meetings for our state arts council. But none of it was considered "gainful employment."

Second, I was insecure because of my father. I respect him and his opinions, but he did not know much about disabled people. He seemed proud of my accomplishments (as a businessman he was impressed with *The Wall Street Journal* article about *The Disability Rag*), but he was not sure that what I did in disability was "work," or that the jobs I have done were the same ones a "real" person would do.

I had pointed out to him many successful disabled people. He thought that was just fine, but "of course, they don't do the same job" a nondisabled person would do. I bragged one day about my friend Alan Farber, who had been appointed judge on the county criminal court.

"That man couldn't possibly be doing the same job as someone who's not disabled," Daddy said. He was sure exceptions were being made for Alan.

"I don't believe so," I said. But Daddy was insistent. He did not question that Alan was a real judge, but he simply could not do the same work as other judges—because he was, of course, handicapped. (Daddy never used that expression, but he would have, if he had thought of it.)

Daddy said people were being nice to us. We were given special treatment. I do not think Daddy would have said that about Franklin D. Roosevelt or about my friends Janet and Ron. Most of my friends did not get "special" treatment at all.

Take Janet, for example. We had been friends since college and both used wheelchairs, but Janet was less disabled than I. If someone met Janet first and then met me, they would never offer to light my cigarette, assuming that, like her, I could open my purse, pull out my cigarette case and lighter, and light my own. I could do most of this except light my cigarette. Usually there was a period of awkwardness as I waited for someone in the group to offer me a light; new people thought I was being coy. On the other hand, if they had met *me* first, they would be all over themselves to be helpful to Janet, handing her a cigarette, reaching to light it, things Janet was perfectly capable of doing on her own.

Janet lived on her own. She drove. She had a real job with the public schools, and it was hard work. Often she had to go to a number of meetings in one day, which meant getting in and out of her car several times. And that meant getting out of her wheelchair and into the car: locking the wheels with the hand brakes; pulling an arm rest out of the socket; pitching it into the back seat—not too far to reach later; pushing her lower body out of the chair and into the driver's seat; reaching out around the door and tugging at the wheelchair until it folded up; pulling the wheelchair up and working to shove it in the back seat, little wheels up, hoping they do not catch on the seat, all the while making sure the seatbelt is not tangled around the wheels; and, finally, getting the door closed. Later, at her destination, she had to repeat the entire procedure in reverse.

She told me about a day when her last meeting was at a high school. When she arrived, the school day had long ended and the place looked deserted. The people she had to meet knew she was coming, but they were inside. She drove her car around the school twice looking for a curb ramp so she could get onto the sidewalk to get in the building once she parked and got out. She found none.

She decided to park and get out of her car anyway. There she sat, in her wheelchair, next to her car, for fifteen minutes, hoping someone would notice before she would have to get herself back into the car, fold and put away her wheelchair, and drive around looking for an accessible pay phone to call the people in the office. Finally, the school principal realized she was late for the meeting and ran out to look for her.

To my question, "Why didn't you ask them if they were accessible before you went?" she replied that she often does not ask because people usually do not know whether their buildings are accessible or not. And, even when they think they know, she cannot rely on them. This time, she said, she *had* called ahead. "The principal told me the school was ramped and insisted I would have no problem getting into the building. He forgot about the four-inch curb I had to get up before I ever got to the ramp."

Ron is another example of a disabled person who got no special treatment on the job. I met Ron, an engineer, when he was featured in an article in *The Disability Rag* on people who tinkered on their own wheelchairs to keep them in working order. Since he had polio in the Fifties, we probably went to Warm Springs at the same time. I am sure he was one of those teenage boys who careened down the hill at top speed shouting, "Runaway chair! Get outta the way!" When I asked him why he would stand with crutches on a pitching and rolling oil barge in the middle of the ocean, Ron said, "Quite honestly, it's because I needed my job."

Sitting in the wheelchair he now used, with his flannel shirt, his beard, and his pipe, he reminded me of Paul Bunyan. "We were doing quite a bit of work on offshore oil drilling and production rigs in the Gulf of Mexico in the Seventies for companies like Shell Oil, Mobil and Gulf," he told me. On one of his trips to Houston calling on contractors for troubleshooting, he said, "The engineers asked me if I would go out to a jack-up drilling rig in the Gulf that had been built using some of our products.

"I said 'sure,' for many reasons—not the least of which was I needed my job, and my company would have taken exception to my saying 'no'," he went on. "I didn't remember that when I stepped out of the helicopter and off the landing pad, I would be stepping onto a gridwork of steel with one-by-three-inch openings to the sea below.

"I was using braces and crutches to walk then. My crutch tip, the part that touches the ground, is three-quarters of an inch in diameter—so it immediately gave way, allowing my long, Warm

Springs-style crutch to go straight down through the grid until the fork of the crutch just below my hand stopped it—leaving me doing a forced one-hand handstand and looking at the sea 150 feet below."

Workers helped him up, and his numbed left arm and shoulder recovered. To solve his problem, he had a worker on the rig put two pins in the crutches about an inch above the end and attach two old orifice plates (big washers, only more expensive) on the bottoms. This, he said, allowed his crutches to act and look like ski poles and prevented them from going through the grid again. "That experience was like a war incident to me. It nearly scared me to death," Ron confided. "But I clanked on—to get the job done."

Janet and Ron made good livings, but I would never be able to work the way they did. I was glad I wanted to be a teacher or a writer, and all I needed was someone to help me potty, bathe, dress, and get in my chair and out the door. Now, with resources like buses and Juanita, I was ready to go for it.

So I began on a serious journey to employment, but on the way, my life began to change dramatically. I guess you could say my life became too normal; it began to get in the way.

For instance, family began to get in the way. By now it was the late eighties, and Daddy had sold most of his rental property and truly retired to his cottage at Lake Cumberland. My move to Kenwood made me much more accessible to him, so I still worked for him. When he came to Louisville, he stayed here. (My brother, M.C., and I joked that he got custody of Mom and I got custody of Daddy; it was lucky our sister, Ann, did not live in town, because we had run out of parents.)

Sometimes Daddy came to Louisville to go to the doctor; he was more conscious of his health and quit smoking on his own. Sometimes he came for business or to meet old buddies for lunch. Often he came for dental work.

When I had lived at home with my parents, many mornings

Daddy would get up early so he could go to the dentist before work. He had dentures on top and permanent false teeth on the bottom, and something always needed fixing or adjusting or redoing. One of the worst things about his family's being poor, Daddy used to say, was not having proper dental care as a child. (I inherited Mom's good teeth—but Daddy's thin hair.)

By now, Michael and Juanita had switched roles; Juanita had moved in and become my full-time personal assistant. Michael still lived here but only worked for me part-time.

When Daddy stayed with me, Juanita offered to sleep on the living room couch so he could sleep on the second floor, which she had turned into a bedroom and sitting room. Michael had made the basement a makeshift studio and apartment. I did not realize until Daddy spent the night that Juanita had taken the mattress off her bed and put it on the floor of her sitting room so she could watch TV "in bed." When I asked Daddy the next morning how he had slept, he said okay except that it was kind of hard getting up off the floor. I apologized.

Having Daddy stay here played into my plan to revitalize this Kenwood house and make it a home again. I wanted to emulate my mom, a charter member of the Kenwood Hill Homemakers Club and a member of the Jefferson County Homemaker Association, the Kentucky Federation of Homemakers, the National Home Demonstration Council, and the International Associated Country Women of the World.

The goal of the Kenwood Hill Homemakers Club, their handbook says, is "to extend to homemakers the opportunity to study homemaking problems under trained leadership, to increase their skill, add to their information, develop their appreciation to the end that they may apply the contribution of science and art to their chosen profession, homemaking, and may more effectively contribute to the well-being of their communities." Each month the group met in someone's home; the hostess and a partner prepared the food for lunch. (Chris helped Mom when it was here.) Members were responsible for attending classes and bringing information back to the other members. Often a county extension agent would attend the meetings. It was a coffee klatch, but with educational opportunities.

Each meeting introduced a major project that could take months to complete: the care and cleaning of sewing machines, making kid gloves, repairing spring cushions, researching your genealogy and illustrating your family tree in crewel embroidery, Swedish darning, and landscaping. Minor projects included one-dish meals, proper posture, furniture arranging, landscaping, book reports, reports on studies on child training (Mom did that), and crafts like making floating candles and Swiss cheese candles (put ice cubes in the mold before you pour in the wax). Martha Stewart's mom was probably a Homemaker.

Mrs. Lynch, one of mother's Homemaker friends, told me years later that Mom taught her how to give a book report. "I was not like most of the others," she said. "I did not read much and I had never given a book report before. But your mom took time with me and helped me prepare. I really appreciated that." My mom was being a teacher.

Most of my life I wanted to be just like my mother, or like what she tried to be. This house felt like Mom, so I was going to try and do Mom stuff. With Juanita's willing help, I could.

Juanita liked helping Daddy, too. (She was less liberated than I was.) I was now his personal assistant, and I liked feeling I could do something for him. On his rare visits, I wanted to make a home for him. Once Juanita and I went all out: hors d'oeuvres on the patio—celery sticks, carrots, radishes, green onions, Benedictine, party rye bread, the kind of snacks Mom used to make most Sunday afternoons. For dinner we had spinach salad, artichoke quiche (an experiment—he said it was good), ham, and potato salad. Juanita also made mint iced tea, which Daddy did not consider a manly drink. "It's very refreshing." he admitted. "But it would be better with bourbon and toss out the tea."

The day after our feast, after Daddy doctor's appointment, after the bank and the store and the pharmacy, Juanita and I helped him pack up to go back to Jamestown and managed to sneak a big piece of quiche into the ice chest. As was his habit, my father called after he arrived back at the cottage. "What a happy surprise! I was tired, I didn't feel like cooking, and I opened the ice chest and voila!" Real men *will* eat quiche if it's fixed for them.

He sent me a note with my bimonthly check, thanking me again. When I told my counselor, Julie, at the Center about it, she said, "Oh, you sound just like a 1950s housewife." I smiled with satisfaction until I realized she didn't mean it as a compliment.

I am sure being a homemaker for Daddy inspired me to try to get Mom to move back to Kenwood—with me. I always thought Mom and I would end up living together, although I had never envisioned *me* taking care of *her*. But we are family, and if Juanita got overloaded, we could hire someone parttime.

There was also the question of economics. Daddy was partially responsible for three households: his (totally) and Mom's and mine (partially). Daddy thought the move was a great idea, but Mom wanted no part of it. Parents do not want to live with their kids, for all kinds of reasons. I am sure it is hard to come back to your house and see someone else living there. But I thought the issue for my mom was that I was using the large bedroom—her bedroom. I don't know how big a person I would have had to be to move back into my old bedroom, but I was not that big.

My alternative idea was to build a separate apartment over a new garage—Mom's own place, not something I had taken over. I had a contractor draw up blueprints for a totally accessible addition right beside the house—a big bedroom and sitting area, a breakfast room/kitchen area, a bathroom—and we would share an entry hall. We would be separate but nearby. Juanita could clean, cook, and do laundry for Mom, or she could hire her own person. Mom was not happy with this idea either, and Daddy panned it because it was too expensive. Since he had never authorized the three hundred dollars for the blueprints, I had to pay for them myself.

In the meantime I had made real efforts to work. Since much of my advocacy experience had been with arts groups, I had developed good relations with our state arts council. While not all arts council people "have the spirit" as Irwin Pickett does, they do believe art is a right, not a privilege, and they try to hold people accountable for any lack of access to the arts. I was a member of the Kentucky Arts Council's standing Civil Rights Advisory Committee (CRAC), established in the early 1980s; disability advocates had been working with the arts council since the 1970s.

The advisory committee advised on compliance with Title 6 of the Civil Rights Act of 1964, Title 9 of the Education Amendments of 1972, Section 504 of the Rehabilitation Act of 1973, and (after 1990) the Americans with Disabilities Act. The committee's job was to "ensure that all citizens shall benefit equally and fully without regard to race, color, creed, religion, national origin, age, sex or disability. And, further, . . . that grantees represent in their programs, staff, board and audience diverse populations." CRAC members served on panels as advisors, reviewed grants, and made recommendations to the KAC Board regarding policies and procedures. We also helped conduct technical assistance workshops to make sure fledgling groups knew what was expected of them.

The technical assistance workshops refreshed my knowledge of grant writing, board organizing, and resource development. It was a lot like VISTA training with a focus on art. I learned that lobbying for arts issues is a lot like lobbying for disability issues: Legislators do not understand either one.

Because I was involved with the arts, I got to meet people like Alberta Allen, the president of the board of the Louisville Orchestra, who had said, "Let's do it" to our request to provide more wheelchair seating at the Macauley Theater. And I met Inez Segell, a member of the board of the Kentucky Arts Council and later appointed to CRAC. Both women had fathers who used wheelchairs. When they saw me, they saw a real person first—a disabled person doing what normal people do.

I first met Inez when members of CRAC—including Gerry Gordon-Brown and me—went to Owensboro, Kentucky, to attend a board of directors meeting of the Kentucky Arts Council. We thought it was important to be there because Janet Rodriguez, program director for special constituencies and staff to the committee, was giving a report about the reorganized committee and the work we had done educating arts groups with workshops on access and compliance. We recommended that the KAC reaffirm its commitment to compliance by stating that it would withhold funds from those not in compliance with civil rights standards. They did, to our great relief; our work to educate would be for naught if arts groups ignored compliance. The KAC had the big stick we needed.

When our part of meeting was over, Inez ran up to us. "What a wonderful report! By the way, I've set it up so that the board will have lunch at this great restaurant. There's plenty of room. You all must join us." I was not interested in going. Restaurants are always crowded, and there is seldom much room for wheelchairs. But I was only one voice, and Inez would not take no for an answer. On the ride over to the restaurant, others filled me in about Inez. She was married to a businessman, well off, and supported the arts through money and volunteering.

Inez seemed thrilled when we arrived. Most people are awkward around me— not Inez; she hugged me and guided me to her table, then buzzed from table to table to make sure everyone was getting what they needed.

Inez insisted I sit at her end of table. Friendly and talkative, she made sure everyone was included in the conversation. I was a little intimidated by arts people, because they know a lot I neither know nor want to know about art. I am an artist in my soul and in my avocation and had a minor in art in college, but I am not knowledgeable about opera, ballet, lots of visual art, folk art, and so on.

Inez said to me, apropos of nothing, "Dear, you have beautiful eyes, but you must let me do your makeup sometime."

"I'm wearing makeup," I stammered.

"Oh, I know, dear. And you do a beautiful job. But you have wonderful eyes and you need to bring them out more." Let me describe Inez: she is short with short black hair and dark eye makeup; she wore dark clothes with a bright red scarf, large gold jewelry, and a hat.

She was getting a little personal, I thought. I needed help to get dressed but I could always put on my own makeup. Was she just being friendly, conversational? Riding home I asked if I should have been offended that she got so personal. Everyone laughed at me. "Is this your first experience with a Jewish mother?" they asked.

When Inez was appointed to the Civil Rights Advisory Committee, we got to know each other better. She took the appointment seriously and learned all about accessible arts, including programing such as audio description (via an FM headset, actors off-stage fill in visual elements of a performance for disabled patrons during natural pauses in the dialogue) and amplification systems (infrared hearing devices that work independently, or in conjunction with, standard hearing aids).

She commented in a CRAC meeting about how great these programs were. "You know, I have friends who are getting older, and after years of coming to arts events, supporting arts events, they quit coming to the plays and the opera because they could no longer see and hear so well. I told them about audio description and the headsets for hearing and now they are coming back!"

"They are using these programs?" I asked.

"Yes. They are so happy to be coming back."

"They would not consider themselves disabled, would they?" I asked.

"No," Inez admitted.

So accessibility also serves people who don't consider themselves card-carrying disabled folks.

Our arts council had great intentions in the 1980s and, like most groups, did its share of backsliding over the years. But I always admired the KAC's efforts toward diversity. The Council did what was necessary to assure the participation of artists and diverse populations. For instance, the Council hired a Yellow Cab van and driver for the day when we went to the board meeting in Owensboro. I felt badly because everyone else could have carpooled less expensively—in a car. Instead, everyone met at my house and the van left from here—expensive car pooling.

The KAC felt we had valuable experience and our time was valuable, so they paid us an honorarium—$125 a day. I was worth $125 a day, plus expenses! That might be a piddling amount to some people, but it was big money to me. And it made me want to do a good job.

Once the arts groups started becoming accessible, the Kentucky Arts Council began asking, Where are disabled people? The arts groups were not seeing much of an increase among patrons with disabilities. I reminded them that they hadn't been accessible before, so how were disabled people to know they were now? The KAC said we had to help by doing a project for the arts groups in Louisville that would bring people with disabilities to performances, an audience development project.

The Council kept asking me about getting this project under way, and I kept making excuses. I was involved with the Advocado Press, publisher of *The Disability Rag*, and had been working on such arts projects as a technical assistance newsletter and resource guide. Since I was designated the arts person at the press, it would be my job to implement any arts programming. I was over my own negative feelings about being with disabled people, but I still did not want to gather "ten or more people" to get a group rate and go anywhere. Most people, most friends, do not go places in groups of ten. I was not interested in a "here come the crippled folks" kind of activity. I offered other ideas, like advertising access and special mailings, getting the word out early, since many people with disabilities have to plan way ahead.

Alberta Allen became the unwitting impetus for the audience development project. She and I had written to each other periodically, just keeping in touch. I often talked to her about fundraising and she would encourage me: "Just ask people, call them, meet with them, talk about your program, ask for what you need, then follow up. Just do it." I could not raise money that way; I never could bring myself to just ask. She called me one day to announce, "Cass, I'm going to Italy for the summer."

"Oh, how nice!"

"Yes. I have tickets to the Louisville Orchestra concerts at the zoo, three tickets to each of the three performances. Would it help you if I gave them to you?" She was aware of our efforts to get people to art events.

"Oh, my goodness. Yes! Thank you!"

These tickets initiated our experimental audience development plan. I contacted friends and acquaintances to ask if they would like to go—and could they pay a share? I do not think people value things as much if they get them for free. Besides, disabled people have money. We can pay our way, although often we cannot pay full price. Everyone chipped in, and with those nine tickets as a start, we were able to take thirteen people to the concerts at the zoo.

Thanks to Alberta's donation, we found that our concept of an audience development program was workable. And, thanks to my friend Martha's donation, I got a part-time office assistant who could help me carry out the work of developing the program.

So I made the arts council a proposal I could live with, the KAC funded it, and we started an audience development project to take people with disabilities to art events—often it was their first time. The project provided tickets, and we had volunteer escorts, peers (disabled people) who were experienced in traveling with first-time patrons. Access to the Arts (A2A) started as a project of the Advocado Press. Our goal was to overcome the final barriers between disabled people and art.

Because of this project and my disability arts experience, I started getting gigs all over the state and making a little money. I needed a van, and a wheelchair-using friend was selling one with a lift. We started getting grants for Access to the Arts, so I was able to keep my office assistant—who drove.

I always had to ask Daddy for anything extra, and a van was a very big extra. I waited for the appropriate moment, reasoned arguments ready: I could become more employable; I would be less of a burden to him (I did *not* use that word). When reasoning failed, as it usually did, I poured out my heart. Daddy had ignored many of my requests. Sometimes he explained the way the world works and how money doesn't buy what it used to, or, as in this case, he told me to wait. I let some time go by and tried again. And again. The van—transportation—was important to me.

Finally, he bought my friend's van. It was red, and I named her Scarlet. Looking back, I am sure Daddy knew then that his health was failing. With a van I could go to Cumberland to see him. Then my office assistant quit for a full-time job, so I lost my driver. Michael had headed west to seek his fame and fortune. Juanita said she could drive but had no license, only a driver's permit. Not my van, I thought.

Sometimes I think of myself as a small business: Juanita was my personal assistant; Claudette was a friend and part-time personal assistant; Jewell's nephew-in-law cut the grass; I even had someone make skirts for me. And now I was looking for a driver again, for only about three days a month.

With my experience, you might think hiring would get easier. It doesn't. I am not comfortable saying, "I need someone to wash my body, but I can only pay minimum wage," and hearing, "I can go work for a fast-food place for more."

I had two people in mind: Arthur Campbell's sister Sue Davis, and Becky Garrett's brother, John Garrett. Sue was in Arthur's movie *If I Can't Do It, It Ain't Worth Doing;* she had experience with Arthur and personal assistance, so I knew she would not be put off by the extra paraphernalia of wheelchairs, tie-downs, lifts on vans, and so forth. Besides, I wanted to get to know her better.

I had known Becky Garrett and her brother John for years. For a while when she was unemployed, Becky lived with Michael and me and we all traveled together. She was like a little sister. John, Michael's best friend, came to the country and spent hours with Michael listening to music, having deep discussions about music, the earth, atoms. They studied astrology. They solved the world's problems.

I was not sure I liked John. He, like Michael, was an Aries. Michael was fast, John frenetic. I did not need to be around two Aries

But John had a good reputation. He had baby-sat for Michael's brother Perry and his wife for several years, and he had worked for my friend Nancy Sullivan, who hired him mostly because he knew me (I had a good reputation too). One of the first things John did for Nancy, quadriplegic as a result of muscular dystrophy, was attach strings to drawers and the refrigerator handle so she could open them and get what she needed herself. John believes in ease of operation. Since the Muscular Dystrophy Association gave Nancy only thirty-five dollars a year to pay for personal assistance services, she paid John out of her own pocket, and he often stayed longer than she could pay him. He almost gave up personal assistance work when she died.

To take a brief detour into what life was like for many disabled people before Kentucky had a Personal Care Attendant Program, look at Nancy's life. Nancy had the services of a home health agency for personal assistance, but they came only four hours a day: two hours in the morning to get her pottied, bathed, dressed, and up in her wheelchair for the day, and two hours in the evening to do the reverse. Agency aides wanted to be done with you and home before dark. Nancy's evening aide wanted her pottied and in bed by seven o'clock, taken care of until morning, with food in reach, the phone nearby, and TV controls on her bed. Nancy lived in public housing. She left her front door unlocked in case she needed someone in between aides.

In my quest for a driver, I called both Sue Davis and John Garrett and left messages. John called me back first. He was working for Leroy as a personal assistant, but he felt he could take a day off or work a half day when I needed him. He seemed interested in the job, but I explained that I had contacted someone else and should talk to her too before making a decision. Sue never called me back.

First, John drove me to Frankfort and back for all-day workshops. He usually returned to Louisville, worked for Leroy (who let him come late), and headed back to Frankfort in the late afternoon to pick me up. As I got to know John, I found I liked him. When I let him keep the van overnight, I knew I was comfortable with him and trusted him. I could not use the van without a driver, and John and his wife, Nancy, had a four-year-old son, Erik, and one car. This way, John would not be without a car while his wife worked third shift. You start thinking about things like that when a child is involved.

Besides, if John had the van, he could come over after working for Leroy and do things for me, like battery maintenance for my wheelchair. Everyone hated that chore; I had been pretty freaked out when I was dependant on Juanita to do it. As Maw-Maw often said, "It's good to have man around."

And John and I ran around in the van. Sometimes I went to the hardware store with him, especially if he was getting stuff for my house. Sometimes we went to the park, sat and talked, and watched the sun go down. Sometimes I just watched him scrub floors or wash the van or pull branches out of the ditch to prevent the ditch from overflowing and seeping into the basement. I learned a great deal about him—not the John of Michael's or Becky's version, but my own. He, like my dad, grew up poor. He was pretty frugal, like Daddy, but he did not stop by the roadside as my dad did to pick up an empty paint can, or a spool of wire, or a good piece of lumber. John was knowledgeable about gas prices and van maintenance, and he liked to tell me how I could save money.

When we were in Lexington one afternoon for an arts council CRAC meeting, we decided to window-shop for a while and eat dinner before we headed home. There was an antique store with gorgeous furniture—a roll top desk, lots of oak furniture, and a beautiful long, narrow pink rug with light blue and white flowers along the edges, perfect for my dining room. We found an art store with all kinds of glass and visual art.

We also were looking for a place to eat. The hotel restaurant was too expensive and we were not dressed up enough. We weren't interested in places that served beer, since we had to drive back to Louisville. The mall had a couple of delicatessens and fast-food places, as well as an ice cream shop with sandwiches. We had to traverse the mall several times before we made up our minds. Sometimes John rode on the back of my chair, as I let certain people do, and I liked the feel of him leaning behind me.

Michael had been gone for months. He and I had been together for fourteen years, even though the last two years had been a process of separating. Now here was John, a real personal assistant who likes the job and housework and pretty yards. How could I not dream?

Three months later, John and I were living together. He and his wife had grown apart, but, like Michael and me, it took them a while to separate. A year earlier, Becky had offered to take John and Erik into her apartment, but John felt her one-bedroom place was too small for two adults, two cats, and a three-year-old child.

I gave John refuge from the storm. Soon he wanted to be with *me*. I told him I gave us two years; by then, I was sure, one of us would come to our senses. I told Daddy that John possibly could be "the one."

John removed the big barriers to my working. I was able to travel again; I could have a career. I just had to try it.

We traveled to CRAC meetings throughout Kentucky, and I attended a two-day civil rights workshop at a state park lodge, chosen partly because it was considered accessible to disabled people—there was much more compliance now with Section 504 of the Rehab Act of 1973. The committee wanted to make sure I was accommodated. (Physical accommodation was such an *interesting* aspect of disability rights.) Determined not to miss any of the next morning's meeting, I got up early. The only accessible entrance to the dining room was in the back of the kitchen, so to have breakfast, I would have to navigate through two sets of doors and dining room tables and chairs. I skipped breakfast. (That is one of the tricks that helps us appear to be doing what nondisabled people do: we skip things like breakfast, sleep, potty breaks, to be sure to be on time.)

I headed for the meeting room. To get there, I had to go outside and up a hill to the sidewalk to the main entrance, go through the lodge's automatic doors and across the main lobby, go out another door that was not automatic, and cross a little bridged walkway. I wondered why the state park system, which understood that an automatic door would be useful for the main lodge, did not seem to think that anyone who needed an automatic door would ever want to get to the meeting rooms.

I went to the front desk and asked the woman behind it if someone could open the door for me. She called maintenance. About a minute later, a man in a park uniform came and escorted me to the walkway. As he opened the door, he told me that just the day before, he had put the makeshift ramp across the threshold. We crossed the breezeway to the meeting room, whose closed door he had to open for me as well.

"Wait a minute, don't go!" I called as he turned to leave. At nearly five minutes past our scheduled starting time, the room was empty. Had he closed the door with me inside, I would have been unable to get out. I told the man I would go back to the lobby and wait. As we crossed the porch, Barbara, another committee member, rushed up, exasperated, afraid she was late. She was as surprised as I was to see no one else around. We decided they must still be in the dining room downstairs at breakfast. In the lobby, she took the stairs down to check, while I remained at the top looking down. I could see the other committee members, all sitting at a large table in the corner. They were not rushing; they were having a conversation. They were, I suspected, getting into the issues I had gotten up so early not to miss.

I wondered what I looked like to them, sitting at the top of the stairs. A couple of them saw me and waved. I moved back quickly. I did not want them to think, Oh, my, Cass is up there; we should do something. I did not want them to feel bad.

It would be rude to complain now that so much access was being provided, now that things were so much better than before. And yet, what nondisabled people did not want to see was that, despite the changes, society was still not accessible to us. Allowances had been made, in their view.

Disabled people now had what Paul Longmore calls "provisional acceptance." We were being accommodated, given special treatment. Longmore blames my hero, Franklin Delano Roosevelt, who he says struck a bargain with society: He did not make his disability a problem for anyone. FDR made a conscious effort to re-enter public life in an acceptable manner—he walked. And society said, We'll accept you, we'll let you stay. Roosevelt's bargain, said Longmore, could only be struck in a society that viewed disability as a transgression, something the disabled person could, with effort, "manage" and control. Disabled people could not complain, could not whimper, and certainly could not protest. That was not part of the bargain.[2]

If I told my fellow committee members that what had happened that morning was discriminatory, they would have said I was overreacting, or I was being too sensitive. It was not conscious discrimination. Nobody *planned* to leave me out. But it happened anyway, because of the way things are.

2. Mary Johnson, "The Bargain," *The Disability Rag*, September/October 1989, 5.

People believed that a disabled person's problems were not related to the denial of rights: They were just their own problems. They were medical problems because of the disability, not problems with discrimination, with denial of accommodation. Sitting above, looking down, I did not accept that analysis anymore. Perhaps because this was a civil rights committee meeting, I felt the discrimination especially acutely. Or perhaps I felt that way because we had spent the previous day in lengthy discussions on prejudice, on discrimination, on being left out.

To join the others, I would have to go out of the lodge, around the building, down the path to the ground floor, back in through another automatic door, and down the hall through the kitchen. By now the committee members were marching up the stairs. The chair of the committee was smiling. "Why didn't you join us for breakfast?"

I smiled back. "I wasn't hungry."

This experience was most enlightening for me. If I got a real job, I could have days like this all week, and I was exhausted after just two. It reminded me of the commercial about the importance of an education that showed a foot race in which one runner was wearing concrete boots. He tried to run with athletes who did not wear concrete boots, and, of course, he lost. He barely crossed the finish line and collapsed from exhaustion. The moral of the story was that a lack of education slows you down, handicaps you. I had a master's degree and about fifteen years of experience, and I was as exhausted as if I had been racing in concrete boots. If this was what a real job was like, I could not handle it.

At home I griped to Janet, the only person who could understand my perspective. That is when she told me her story about the after-school meeting at the inaccessible accessible school. She dealt with that kind of thing daily. I could not.

It became obvious that if I wanted to be employed "like everyone else," I was going to have to adapt a job to what I could do. I could work part-time, and I could put in additional hours if I could work at home. So I got more involved with arts programming, including writing grants.

I worked on projects like the Kentucky *Disabled Artist Directory*, a list of artists with disabilities, and *Open to All*, a resource guide and artist directory. The audience development project, A2A, was doing well; we had three escorts taking people to art events. I hired John as an administrative assistant for A2A. Juanita was our star volunteer; she stapled papers, folded letters, stuffed envelopes, and helped me set up escorts meetings.

Our work was well received. One grants reviewer commented, "This someday could grow to be a $100,000 organization." And I thought, No! Wait! I don't think I want to work that hard.

Whenever we could during my travels for work, John and I swung by Lake Cumberland to see Daddy. By now, he was not coming to Louisville often, and he listed Jamestown, Kentucky, as his home. Sadly, when he finally retired for real, when he was free to travel or do whatever he wanted, his health began to fail. Considering his lifestyle, no one was surprised.

Daddy began smoking in his teens. He smoked cigarettes, cigars, and pipes. As a teenager, he worked at Porter Paint cleaning out paint cans (before we worried about the chemicals in paint). After college he worked in Porter's chemistry labs. He ate meat, the redder the better. He drank a lot for years. For him *not* to have health problems at his age would have been a miracle.

Daddy and Mother had always coughed. Mom said she was allergic to dust; we thought she did not want to do the house-cleaning herself. But Daddy's cough got worse. He had trouble breathing and he tired easily. His Louisville doctors talked about allergies, asthma (Daddy scoffed at that), and emphysema. They hospitalized him and scoped his lung. At first they thought he had inhaled something like a peanut skin that irritated his lung. In fact, he had chronic obstructive pulmonary disease (COPD).

What should we do? M.C., who had a car, had visited Daddy at Cumberland, taken supplies, fished or water skied, and done chores for Daddy when he could. Now I had a van (and John and Juanita), so going to Cumberland became my responsibility, too. I had not gone since Daddy had retired and moved down there full-time three years earlier. John and I planned a first visit, check the place out, and see what he needed and what we could do for him. Because of the art gigs, I was able to say, "Don't worry, Daddy, they're paying for the gas!"

From Louisville to Jamestown is an uneventful drive, mostly country. Talking was hard because my wheelchair tie-downs are in the middle of the van, so I am behind the driver. Add road noises and it is almost impossible to communicate. We listened to music. Past Jamestown, I had to direct John to our cottage. We turned off the main road onto Scott's Chapel Road, named for a little straight narrow white box of a building with a steeple that no longer existed.

Once on Scott's Chapel Road, I found giving directions a challenge. Some of these old country roads went to only one home; some took steep turns downhill; some looked dark and dangerous. One of the first things Daddy did after we got the cottage was make signs to point the way. He was not the only one. There were at least half a dozen signs of one kind or another at each intersecting road. Most were homemade; a couple looked as through they were made in shop class. Several had sparkles.

Daddy's signs were small, close to the ground, inconspicuous orange-and-cream arrows made out of old Porter Paint cans. He put reflective paint on them and mounted them at every intersection or confusing part of the route to our cottage, but you had to be looking for them to notice them. On dark nights when we left Louisville too late and got to Cumberland after dark, those reflective Porter Paint arrows were the most welcoming of signs.

When my family first started going down to Cumberland in the 1960s, these roads were not paved. Most people here lived on tiny family farms with a little tobacco and corn, a vegetable garden, chickens, and a cow. A widow with a true family farm, Mrs. Keane, lived in a small house near the road you turned onto to get to our cottage. Our one-lane road served us, our neighbors from Cincinnati, and anyone who had to get to Granny Spring, the source of our water. The first time I went down that road, I was concerned about someone coming the other way, and Daddy said, "You just pull over and let them pass." I looked out the car window and saw no *over*. If you pulled over, you'd fall off the road and slide down the hill into the lake.

John was not comfortable coming down our road for the first time either, even though it was daylight. Then the circular driveway to the cottage kind of unnerved him. I mistakenly told him to turn in the wrong way, so when we got to the bottom of the drive, our van was facing the other vehicles in the driveway.

Daddy had been building onto the cottage, and two trucks were parked in the drive along with Daddy's Blazer. As I got out, a builder came out of the cottage saying, "Wait, I have to put the ramp down." Although Daddy had assured me he had built a ramp from the driveway down to the cottage, what he had actually done was a lot cheaper. He covered the steps with a piece of plywood reinforced with a couple of two-by-fours; it gave when I rolled down it, and it was so steep John had to pull back on my chair to keep me from rolling too fast. People could not even walk down it comfortably. I knew Daddy had made it that way so he could move it. If he were rich, Daddy would have made a permanent, safe, regulation ramp.

The first thing Daddy said when we got inside was: "Why did you pull in backwards? Didn't you see the trucks?" No hello, no how are you.

"Hi, I'm John. Cass told me to pull in that way."

After Daddy finished up with the builders, he showed us around. Granny's Villa, as he had named it, was no longer a summer cottage. The first thing he did when he moved there permanently was install a better heating and air conditioning system. He doubled the size of the kitchen, adding room for a table and chairs. He added an office and a master bedroom. He needed the space for the furniture from his Louisville home and the furniture a lady friend gave him when she moved from a house to a condo. His plan when he retired was to share his home with one of two women, but it was not to be. I know they both loved him and Cumberland but they had grown older, too.

More rooms, more furniture, more clutter, more work, and Daddy could not do it all anymore. He needed a wife or a personal assistant, someone to make life easier. Still, he was not alone. He had become pretty well known in Jamestown. He made friends easily, told jokes with the guys (or worse, stories of his conquests), flirted with the women and made them blush and feel special in a good way. He visited the Senior Citizens Center at lunchtime looking for companionship, and he found lady friends, platonic and otherwise, but he had not found a partner. He had some help from a husband and wife who cleaned his house, did the laundry, and helped in the garden. One of our chores was to bring cases of beer to him to assure his helpers would show up. (Jamestown was in a dry county.) Daddy knew he would not see them for days once he gave them the beer, but he made them work for it.

John and I stayed for the day to assess the situation and see what we could do to help. Since we were in the driveway backward, John had to turn the van around before we could leave. Somehow—probably because Daddy was watching and giving advice—the van slipped off the drive and slid into a small tree and got stuck.

"Why did you do that?" Daddy hollered. John was mortified. What a thing to do when you are trying to impress someone's father! We had to get Mrs. Keane's grandson and his tractor to pull the van back onto the driveway.

On the way back to Louisville in the dark, I got us lost. The trip took four hours instead of two and a half. When we got home and had some time to unwind, I asked John what he thought of my dad. "He's just like most of the old men I've known," he answered. I was shocked. I had never thought of my dad as old.

When I was a little girl, everyone said Daddy was handsome. He was six feet tall, muscular, and athletic. He had bought the cottage at Lake Cumberland so he could water ski. He played tennis and was a good swimmer and diver, but he never took to golf because it was too slow. He liked to sweat. Daddy had been a playboy in image and in reality, a member of the Playboy Club, always in fashion. His personality was "handsome" too. A southern gentleman, he spoke well and was usually kind. He had singing lessons when he was young and sang in the church choir before he married. When we were little, Mother played piano for the church choir and Daddy was choir director. My friends were always shocked to learn this about my dad; they loved and admired him, but they knew him as a rogue, someone who loved to sing with the piano player at a bar.

My friend Gerry Gordon-Brown especially loved Daddy's voice because she could understand him without her hearing aids. "One of the things I will forever remember about your Dad is his tone of voice, nice and low. I could listen to him forever." Daddy liked that kind of compliment.

Now, with John's help and my gigs, we were able to go to Daddy's about twice a month and stay several days each time. Mostly, we cleaned up and made food; John and Daddy are both good cooks. Sometimes we took Juanita to help.

In the summer of 1991, Daddy got pneumonia, and I knew when he left the hospital he was going to need more help. I called three nurses I knew from my NOW chapter and learned everything I could about his condition and what he could expect. One nurse taught me all about sleep apnea; she wanted him to be in her sleep apnea program in Louisville. He wouldn't go. Another friend suggested a breathing clinic in Bowling Green. He would not do that either.

The one thing I could do was get him home health services. When Daddy left the hospital, he was on oxygen; from home health services, he was eligible for a nurse once a week and home health aides three times a week. He accepted the help more willingly when he found out he did not have to pay for it.

He, like my mother, did not mind people working for him. It was hard on him to be "helpless"; he preferred to think he could still do it all. I remember how I was treated whenever I have approached the medical community: I become a "helpless cripple" incapable of knowing what is right for me, because of either their attitude or my intimidation. I become a patient.

"Patient" connotes a person unable to speak on his or her own behalf. A patient fears not so much lifestyle change as a loss of self. The fear is justified. People who preach cure play into this belief. Everyone will not be cured, but everyone can use personal assistance.

Having home aides was good for Daddy's ego. He was an interesting character, colorful, worldly, and intelligent. He was a good conversationalist and admired for his experiences. People loved talking to him and often asked his advice on everything from sex to gardening. He lectured several nurses about planning for their financial futures. Everyone, of course, thought he was handsome.

He enjoyed the visits and the help, although he griped about not being able to do things for himself. He felt he did not need a bath three times a week, because he was not working hard enough to build up a sweat, so he especially griped during the showers. Sometimes he joked with his female aides that it would be fun if they joined him. One day, in a particularly grumpy mood, Daddy muttered through the whole shower. Since he had a new aide that day, John tried to explain that Daddy did not like the state he was in. Her response was, "Mel, you don't like Kentucky?" Daddy looked at John and just rolled his eyes.

He also griped that in thirty days the agency had sent nineteen different aides. Poor planning, he complained. "If the aide has never been here before, they get lost," he complained. "They stop and call me for directions. All that wastes time and gas and wear and tear on their car." I was more concerned that no single person was seeing him on a regular basis. How could anyone mark a change in his condition?

Since John and I went to his home often, we met many of his aides. Even though they were capable help, it was hard for me to leave Daddy and go back to Louisville. Usually it would be late afternoon, the sun beginning to go down—a beautiful, melancholy time of day. One sunny afternoon I sat on the screened porch talking with Daddy while John loaded the van. Daddy was in his usual place on the porch, in a chair near the back corner, near the deck overlooking the lake. While we talked, I watched hummingbirds come to the feeders hanging from the deck behind his shoulder.

Daddy would complain and then apologize—"I'm not telling you something you don't already know." I was shocked to hear him apologize. He was not used to being "helpless" and did not know what to expect. It was the first time, I think, that he understood what my life had been like. "I need someone like John," Daddy said, and he was right. He needed someone who cared how he was and worked with him to have the best, healthiest life possible. As John and I drove away, I felt pulled in two directions—toward work and toward my dad.

During the Christmas holidays in 1991, Daddy went into the hospital with pneumonia again. This time we did not know if he would come out. If he could get stronger, his doctor said, maybe he could fight it off. But Daddy was very weak and the prognosis grave. He was in the hospital three weeks; John and I went to Cumberland as often as we could, spending most afternoons at the hospital and evenings getting the place ready for when he came home.

He could not live alone anymore. He could not dress himself, get out of bed by himself. I suggested he move back to Louisville to Kenwood so we could take care of him here, but he refused. Cumberland was his home.

If I could have done it by myself, I would have moved down there with him and taken care of him. But I am a quadriplegic, and any taking care of I do is going to be through someone else's hands. Juanita had family in Louisville, and John had his son on the weekends. I could not make such a commitment for them.

We began looking for someone to stay with him. His doctor wanted him stronger before he left the hospital, but Daddy wanted to go home. I think he thought he could manage on his own. I was on the phone for days trying to track down a personal attendant, and finally I got a tentative yes from a woman named Jean.

That night Daddy called from the hospital. He was tired of being there, he told me. They could not help him anymore. He was not going to get any better. I told him the doctor had said he thought he could get Daddy into the next available Medicare bed. That was a big issue with Daddy—expense. But he wanted to go home.

I explained that we did not have anyone yet to stay with him and begged him to wait and talk to his doctor in the morning. He told me he had told his doctor he was checking himself out tomorrow, with or without medical permission. How could I stop him?

Luckily that tentative yes from Jean became a firm agreement, but she could not start for a couple of days. The next day we got up and dressed, finished cleaning up, and got his room ready. About eleven, we got a phone call from the hospital to tell us Daddy was leaving the hospital and on the way home.

We heard the dogs barking way up at Keane's farm, and then Daddy's three dogs chimed in. Daddy arrived in a huge red-and-white ambulance, no flashing lights, no sirens. John had moved our van to the next-door neighbor's drive and parked Daddy's Blazer out of the way. The ambulance pulled in; the doors opened. Even before the stretcher appeared, Daddy was hollering at his dogs to stop barking. The minute they heard his voice, they got more excited. Finally, the attendants slid the stretcher out. There sat my daddy, propped up in a hospital gown, his eyes looking enormous because of his trifocal glasses and his frailty—roaring.

I cannot describe the look on Daddy's face when he saw he was home again. He surveyed his surroundings, told the ambulance drivers what to do, what to get out of the ambulance. He warned them about the ramped steps, pointed out and explained his garden, and finally directed them to his bedroom.

I hate to admit that my dad, far from politically correct when it comes to disability, taught me about language that day. From the beginning of my disability work with ALPHA, I have been involved with language, grappling with words like "invalid," "crippled." Words are so important that *The Disability Rag* came out with consciousness-raising bookmarks that explained why words like "victim," "confined," and "wheelchair bound" are incorrect. Wheelchairs are *not* confining. In fact, I could not go anywhere without mine—unless someone is willing to carry me. "Victim" is an emotional term that conjures up tragedy; the real tragedy is that society does not see us as okay the way we are—disabled. Most terms used for people with disabilities are medical, clinical, derogatory.

One word we have not found a substitute for is "homebound." As a child in the fifties and sixties, when I was considered "homebound," I did not think the label fit. Agencies define homebound people as those who cannot leave home. I could leave home whenever someone would take me.

My friend Sanda Aronson and I have discussed this term at length. Sanda, a visual artist, is founder and executive director of the Disabled Artists' Network out of New York. She has been an art teacher and is a veteran of the feminist art movement of the 1970s. She has an environmental disability, so she does not leave home. She has chronic fatigue syndrome and is an allergic asthmatic. Because society has not figured out how to deal with her disabilities, she is considered "homebound."

My dad taught me a different definition of homebound. That last night when he called me and said he was checking himself out of the hospital, I knew he was determined to be home. He demanded it and he got it. When I saw him pop out of that ambulance I thought, My father is homebound. He was bound and determined to be home.

One week after leaving Daddy with Jean, his live-in attendant, I got a call from his friend Millie, from his house. Jean had called her and said she could not do the work; she was quitting. Millie had been a "girlfriend" of my father's and had helped him in the past, so I asked if she could stay until John and I could get there. Since it was the weekend, we had John's son, Erik, and could not leave Louisville until the next evening, Sunday. Millie said she would stay and we talked awhile about how Daddy was taking all this. "He thinks she quit because she just needed some money, and once she got paid . . ."

Juanita went to Cumberland with us. She was prepared to stay if we did not find a better solution by the next weekend, when we had to return to Louisville to Erik. She liked my dad, who called her Barbara because he thought she looked like a Barbara. Juanita thought that was funny.

With Juanita at Cumberland, John would be totally responsible for my personal assistance at home. John is a good personal assistant and when we went on trips he was my PA, but taking care of both me and Erik on weekends would be hard for him.

Daddy had checked himself out of the hospital to come home to die. When he was still alive a week later, he began asking why was it taking so long. He told John he wanted to go outside and freeze to death. "Mel," John had to tell him, "the low tonight is only going to be forty."

Our worst problem was that Russell County had no hospice service, which meant no one told us what to expect or gave us guidance. Daddy got worse. He still had pneumonia, so he could not breathe well. Nurses and aides came for an hour or two each day, but all they could do was try to make him comfortable. He could never get comfortable.

Daddy began having trouble sleeping and would call out at night. We got a baby monitor, so he could whisper and we could hear him. Soon he began calling out about every twenty minutes, although he did not realize it was that often. Since Juanita, a heavy sleeper, did not wake up, John got up for Daddy all night long and got no sleep. We asked the agency to send someone to stay overnight.

The day Daddy died, Juanita got up early as usual, before Mark, the overnight person, left. John and I got up midmorning; it would be noon before I could get dressed and up in my chair.

By early afternoon, the aide had come and gone. John and I headed for town in the van to run errands. In the middle of the road, close to town, was a cardboard Porter Paint box, open, upside down—in perfect condition.

"John," I said.

"No!" he exclaimed. "We're not going to go back and get it."

"I know, I know. But it is in good shape. We could use a box like that."

He knew I was kidding. We went to the bank on the far side of town, where I went in, and to the store, where I did not have to go in, and to the drugstore. On our way out of town, we passed the Porter Paint box again. It was still in the *middle* of the road, still upside down, still in perfect condition. Evidently, everyone had driven around it.

When we got back to the cottage, Daddy was the same so I decided the Porter Paint box wasn't an omen. At about nine o'clock, Mark arrived. I greeted him, and John walked with him into Daddy's room, filling him in on Daddy's present condition.

I went to the master bedroom and sat by the big window overlooking the lake. The first time we came here, John was excited about the window until we realized it was set so high I could barely see out of it. Now I looked for stars and the moon and thought, How remarkable, I am here with the first most important man in my life, Daddy, and with John, who I hope will be the last most important man in my life.

From Daddy's bedroom over the baby monitor, I could hear John and Mark were mumbling. Then John said quietly but firmly, "Cassie, come in here. *Now.*"

How ironic that most of what I had learned about disability issues, many of the connections I had made, benefited my dad. I had studied all my life, prepared all my life, for this job—daughter. Daddy gave me the resources to have a life and I had given back to him the only way I could.